INTEGRATED MATHEMATICS SCHEME

IMSA1

INTEGRATED MATHEMATICS SCHEME

IMSA1

Peter Kaner

**Formerly Inspector for Mathematics
Inner London Education Authority**

Bell & Hyman · London

First published 1982 by
Bell & Hyman Limited
Denmark House
37–39 Queen Elizabeth Street
London SE1 2QB

Reprinted 1983 (twice), 1984

© Peter Kaner 1982

All rights reserved. No part of this publication may be reproduced, stored in
a retrieval system, or transmitted in any form or by any means, electronic,
mechanical, photocopying, recording or otherwise, without prior
permission of Bell & Hyman Ltd.

Kaner, Peter

    Integrated mathematics scheme.
    Book   A1
    1. Mathematics – 1961–
    I. Title
    510   QA39.2

ISBN 0 7135 1330 6

Typeset by CCC, printed and bound in Great Britain by
William Clowes Limited, Beccles and London

Contents

Acknowledgements

The publishers would like to thank the following for permission to
reproduce photographs:

The Central Electricity Generating Board
The Imperial War Museum
Mr A F Kersting, A.I.I.P., F.R.P.S.
The National Portrait Gallery
The United States House of Representatives (Architect of the Capitol).

Illustrations by Steve Simon.

Unit M1 Use of calculator I

Introducing your calculator

You may be very good at arithmetic. I hope you are. In this book
you are going to save your brain for thinking and use a calculator to
do all the routine work.

To begin with, let us check that you know enough to be able to
start the course.

Exercise M1

Write down the answers to these.

A
1 + 1	2 + 2	3 + 3	4 + 4	5 + 5
6 + 6	7 + 7	8 + 8	9 + 9	10 + 10

B
2 + 5	3 + 4	4 + 5	5 + 7	6 + 7
7 + 0	4 + 8	6 + 9	7 + 8	9 + 5
10 + 3	5 + 10	9 + 10	9 + 8	8 + 6

C
5 − 3	6 − 2	4 − 1	5 − 5	6 − 4
7 − 2	8 − 5	10 − 6	9 − 4	9 − 2
10 − 5	6 − 0	9 − 7	9 − 3	10 − 4

D
2 × 2	2 × 3	2 × 5	2 × 7	2 × 8
4 × 2	5 × 2	10 × 2	6 × 2	0 × 2

E
3 × 3	3 × 5	4 × 5	5 × 5	5 × 6
5 × 7	4 × 6	4 × 8	8 × 6	10 × 3
4 × 10	6 × 3	8 × 5	10 × 7	10 × 9

F
8/2	6/3	15/5	24/6	25/5
40/8	48/8	70/10	36/9	100/10

The sign / is another way of writing ÷. It means 'divided by'. In this book we use both / and
÷.

Exercise M2

1	2	3	4	5	6	7	8	9	10
5	10	15	20	25	30	35	40	45	50

A The above table shows the 5 times multiplication table. Each number in the bottom line is 5 times the number above it.

    1 Make a table for × 3   **2** Make a table for × 4

    3 Make a table for × 6   **4** Make a table for × 8

    Use squared paper.

B Use the four tables you have made to answer these.

    1 3×7 **2** 5×6 **3** 10×8 **4** 8×6

    5 $24/4$ **6** $56/8$ **7** $60/10$ **8** $72/8$

The four-function calculator

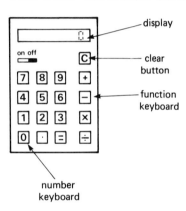

The **display** shows answers.

The **number keyboard** has buttons which put numbers into the machine when you press them.

The **function buttons** add, subtract, multiply or divide the numbers you put into the machine.

I shall use a button sign when I want you to press a button, ☐.

Examples:

⟨on⟩	switch on	⟨=⟩	press the equals button
⟨off⟩	switch off	⟨+⟩	press the plus button
⟨7⟩	press 7	⟨C⟩	press the clear button
⟨7⟩ ⟨2⟩	press 7 and then press 2		

Exercise M3

A Press these: ⟨1⟩ ⟨C⟩ ⟨2⟩ ⟨C⟩ ⟨3⟩ ⟨C⟩ and watch the display.

    What does the ⟨C⟩ button do?

B Put these numbers on the display.

      4   25   33   10   45

      70   77   123   450   206

C What number would you *expect* on the display if you followed these sequences?

1 C 3 2 0   **2** C 2 0 5   **3** C 4 6 8

4 C 0 2   **5** C 0 2 3   **6** C 0 3 0 4

7 C 4 0 0 7   **8** C 0 4 4 0

Check on your calculator.

D **1** What is the largest number you can make on the display?

2 What is the smallest number you can make on the display?

E Put these numbers on the display.

1 48 523	**2** 56 143	**3** 9 090 909	**4** 7 654 321
5 124 680	**6** 335 577	**7** 444 444	**8** 7 000 001

Errors

If you make a mistake in punching the numbers, always clear and start again.

F Find the errors in these.

1 C 9 8 7 6 5 4 3 2 . . . *98675432*

2 C 2 4 6 8 1 3 5 7 . . . *24681257*

3 C 4 0 2 5 6 1 4 5 . . . *40265145*

4 C 1 1 2 3 3 3 0 0 . . . *11223300*

Care of your calculator

READ THESE GOLDEN RULES

1 Never leave it switched on.

2 Never drop it.

3 Never get it wet. (Don't do calculations in the bath!)

4 Don't lend it.

5 Don't push the buttons very hard. A touch is enough.

6 Don't leave it in the hot sunshine or on a radiator.

7 Always check that it is switched off whenever you see it.

Exercise M4

A Try to get these numbers on the display.

1 02	**2** 045	**3** 006	**4** 60 003	**5** blank 3
6 blank 30	**7** blank 2 blank	**8** 5.....5		

Do you agree with these comments?

The calculator will not put a zero in front of a whole number.

You cannot get blanks between numbers, only zeros.

The only place for a blank is in front of a number.

B   Study all the different numbers on the display.

1   Which numbers are made from more strokes than their value? (e.g. ¦, value 1 but made of two strokes.)

2   Which numbers are made from less strokes than their value?

3   Which numbers are made from the same number of strokes as their value?

4   Which numbers are the same upside down?

5   Which numbers are the same back to front?

6   Which numbers make other numbers when they are upside down?

SWITCH OFF

Unit M2   Use of calculator II

Addition

The calculator will add any pair of numbers using the $\boxplus$ and $\boxminus$
buttons.

Example:

$45 + 38$

$\boxed{\text{C}}\ \boxed{4}\ \boxed{5}\ \boxed{+}\ \boxed{3}\ \boxed{8}\ \boxed{=}$

Display   *0   4   45 45   3   38 83*

Fig. 2

$$\begin{array}{r} 45 \\ +\,38 \\ \hline 83 \end{array}$$

Rough check:
$40 + 40 = 80$

You should always have some idea of what to expect, so do a rough
check in your head.

Exercise M5

A   Add these on your calculator. Write in your book the buttons you press and what appears
in the display (as in Fig. 2).

    1 $3 + 5$ **2** $10 + 12$ **3** $33 + 65$ **4** $78 + 90$ **5** $103 + 27$

    6 $154 + 68$ **7** $198 + 72$ **8** $325 + 167$ **9** $485 + 773$ **10** $629 + 789$

B   What sums do these sequences represent? What would you expect the display to show at
the end?

    1 $\boxed{\text{C}}\ \boxed{1}\ \boxed{0}\ \boxed{+}\ \boxed{4}\ \boxed{3}\ \boxed{=}$ **2** $\boxed{\text{C}}\ \boxed{2}\ \boxed{3}\ \boxed{+}\ \boxed{7}\ \boxed{1}\ \boxed{=}$

    3 $\boxed{\text{C}}\ \boxed{3}\ \boxed{2}\ \boxed{0}\ \boxed{+}\ \boxed{5}\ \boxed{8}\ \boxed{5}\ \boxed{=}$ **4** $\boxed{\text{C}}\ \boxed{6}\ \boxed{+}\ \boxed{6}\ \boxed{6}\ \boxed{6}\ \boxed{=}$

C   Look through this list of sums and pick out the answers that are *obviously* wrong. Then
check on the calculator.

    1 $4 + 7 = 10$ **2** $5 + 9 = 12$ **3** $6 + 8 = 14$

    4 $16 + 23 = 39$ **5** $48 + 33 = 251$ **6** $62 + 31 = 91$

    7 $80 + 190 = 276$ **8** $650 + 32 = 75$ **9** $712 + 48 = 760$

    10 $10 + 14 = 27$ **11** $77 + 184 = 261$ **12** $634 + 248 = 882$

    Did you miss any of the 7 mistakes?

D Follow these sequences. Guess what the display will show *before* you work the sequence on the calculator.

1 [C] [3] [+] [5] [+]

2 [C] [4] [+] [6] [+]

3 [C] [1] [4] [+] [1] [0]

4 [C] [5] [+] [2] [5] [+]

5 [C] [4] [+] [6] [−]

6 [C] [1] [+] [1] [2] [−]

7 [C] [2] [0] [+] [3] [3] [−]

8 [C] [4] [2] [+] [2] [5] [−]

9 [C] [6] [+] [3] [×]

10 [C] [7] [+] [1] [0] [×]

11 [C] [5] [+] [4] [÷]

12 [C] [1] [4] [+] [7] [÷]

Calculator rule 1

Given two numbers a and b, the sum $a + b$ is found from the sequence [C] [a] [+] [b] [∗], where ∗ is one of $+$, $−$, $\times$, $\div$ or $=$.

Subtraction

The calculator will subtract any pair of numbers using [C] [a] [−] [b] [=] or generally [C] [a] [−] [b] [∗] where ∗ is any one of $+$, $−$, $\times$, $\div$ or $=$.

Example:

$44 − 21$

[C] [4] [4] [−] [2] [1] [=]

Display *0 4 44 44 2 21 23*

$$\begin{array}{r} 44 \\ -21 \\ \hline 23 \end{array}$$

Rough check:
$40 − 20 = 20$

Exercise M6

A Subtract these on your calculator. Write the programme (which buttons you press) and also write down the numbers that appear on the display.

1 $7 - 4$	**2** $14 - 9$	**3** $27 - 12$	**4** $48 - 22$	**5** $73 - 28$
6 $128 - 66$	**7** $400 - 173$	**8** $562 - 197$	**9** $620 - 77$	**10** $950 - 606$

B What subtractions do these sequences represent? What would the display show at the end of each sequence?

1 [C] [6] [−] [2] [+]

2 [C] [3] [8] [−] [1] [9] [÷]

3 [C] [4] [2] [−] [7] [=]

4 [C] [2] [2] [−] [7] [8] [−]

5 [C] [4] [5] [0] [−] [2] [3] [8] [×]

C Look through this list of subtractions. Pick out the answers that are obviously wrong. Explain why you have picked them out in each case.

Example:
$28 - 16 = 52$
Wrong, because 52 is larger than 28. You have taken 16 away so the result should be smaller.

$10 - 3 = 12$	$20 - 10 = 15$	$35 - 25 = 25$	$40 - 18 = 22$
$85 - 32 = 50$	$120 - 65 = 55$	$133 - 47 = 180$	$270 - 145 = 135$
$408 - 210 = 182$	$300 - 150 = 55$	$667 - 188 = 479$	$65 - 27 = 92$

D What would you expect the calculator to display after these sequences?

1 ☐C☐ ☐2☐ ☐−☐ ☐5☐ ☐=☐   2 ☐C☐ ☐3☐ ☐−☐ ☐7☐ ☐=☐

3 ☐C☐ ☐7☐ ☐−☐ ☐1☐ ☐0☐ ☐=☐   4 ☐C☐ ☐2☐ ☐0☐ ☐−☐ ☐3☐ ☐0☐ ☐=☐

5 ☐C☐ ☐5☐ ☐0☐ ☐−☐ ☐1☐ ☐0☐ ☐0☐ ☐=☐   6 ☐C☐ ☐1☐ ☐0☐ ☐0☐ ☐−☐ ☐2☐ ☐5☐ ☐0☐ ☐=☐

Check through each one and look at the result very carefully.

What do you notice? What is the connection between $3 - 5$ and $5 - 3$?

Calculator rule 2

When the calculator subtracts a *larger* number from a *smaller* number the result is *negative*. (Shown by a − in front of the answer.)

Example:
$2 - 8 = -6$

Calculator rule 3

Given two numbers a, b,
$b - a = -(a - b)$

Example:
$6 - 9 = -(9 - 6)$

Exercise M7

A Check rule 3 for these examples.

1	$4 - 8$	**2**	$6 - 10$	**3**	$9 - 15$	**4**	$24 - 37$
5	$35 - 66$	**6**	$48 - 83$	**7**	$55 - 77$	**8**	$60 - 100$
9	$120 - 250$	**10**	$188 - 254$	**11**	$232 - 401$	**12**	$355 - 728$

B Pick out the obvious mistakes from these. Explain how you picked them out.

1	$14 + 17 = 20$	**2**	$18 - 8 = 10$	**3**	$45 - 23 = 68$
4	$30 + 75 = 105$	**5**	$5 - 18 = 13$	**6**	$6 - 12 = -6$
7	$14 - 23 = 9$	**8**	$100 - 30 = 75$	**9**	$42 - 65 = -107$
10	$143 + 37 = -180$	**11**	$253 + 464 = 717$	**12**	$253 - 464 = -211$

Unit M3 Metric measurement I

Length

The standard unit of length is the **metre**. Abbreviation m.

Example:

A very tall man will be almost 2 metres high.

The metre is divided into 1000 millimetres (mm).

A kilometre (km) is the distance equal to 1000 metres.

1 m = 1000 mm

1 km = 1000 m

Examples:

Lines which are 4 millimetres, 20 millimetres and 145 millimetres in length.

━ 4mm

━━━━━━ 20mm

145mm

━━

Exercise M8

A Use your ruler to measure these lines in mm. Would they make a metre if they were put in one long line?

1 ━━━━━━

2 ━━━━

3 ━━━━━━━━

4 ━━━━━━━━━

5 ━━━━━━━━━━

6 ━━━━━━━━━━━

7 ━━━━━━━

8 ━━━━━━━━━━━

| 9 ———————— | 10 ════════════════ |
| 11 ——— | 12 ═══════════════════ |

B   Which of these measurements are unreasonable?

    1 A giraffe 5 metres high   **2** A tower 1 km high

    3 A snake 10 m long   **4** An insect 3 mm long

    5 Paper 5 mm thick   **6** A road 20 metres long

    7 A house 60 metres high   **8** A river 100 metres across

C   Measure these things. Use the most suitable unit.

    1 Your own height

    2 The length of this book

    3 The width of this book

    4 The thickness of this book

    5 The distance from one corner of the classroom to the opposite corner. (Compare your results with other students.)

    6 The distance from home to school. (Count your 'pace' as about $\frac{3}{4}$ m.)

D   Which of the metric units of length (km, m or mm) would be the most suitable to measure these? Give reasons.

    1 The length of a hockey pitch   **2** The thickness of a piece of paper

    3 A length of material for a shirt   **4** The length of cotton on a reel

    5 The depth of a trench   **6** The height of an aircraft

    7 The distance to the moon   **8** The length of a container lorry

Mass (weight)

The units of mass follow the same pattern as the units of length.

milligram (mg)   gram (g)   kilogram (kg)

1000 mg = 1 g

1000 g = 1 kg

Because the gram is very small, the kilogram is the 'everyday weight' in use in shops. It is known as the kilo for short.

Examples:

A housefly weighs about 10 mg

A normal baby weighs between 2 and 4 kg when it is born

A bag of sugar will be 1 kg or 2 kg

A pencil weighs about 10 g

This book weighs about 300 g

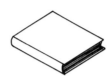

An alsatian dog weighs about 20 kilos

Exercise M9

A Which of these masses (weights) are unreasonable?

1 A baby weighing 35 mg
2 A bird weighing 35 kg
3 A motor car weighing 100 g
4 A chocolate weighing 50 mg
5 A girl weighing 50 kg
6 A teapot weighing 25 kg
7 A cow weighing 400 kg
8 An apple weighing 5 g

B What would you expect these objects to weigh if you weighed them? (If you have scales available you should weigh a number of things to get the 'feel' of 1 kg, etc.)

1 Yourself
2 Your head if it were cut off
3 A wellington boot
4 A woollen glove
5 A paintbrush
6 A 1 cm nail
7 A jam tart
8 Your chair
9 A bucket of water
10 A football (Would it weigh more, less or the same if it were punctured?)

Changing units

It is very simple to change units in the metric system as the figures do not change.

Examples:

(a) 2 kg = 2000 g
(b) 3 m = 3000 mm
(c) 4 km = 4000 m
(d) 5 g = 5000 mg
(e) 0·5 m = 500 mm
(f) 1·5 kg = 1500 g

Exercise M10

A Change these measures to a smaller unit.

1 3 kg
2 4 m
3 5 km
4 6 g

5 0·5 kg	**6** 0·4 m	**7** 0·6 km	**8** 0·3 g
9 1·2 kg	**10** 2·5 m	**11** 4·3 km	**12** 6·2 g

B Write these measurements out in full, e.g., 4 g = 4 grams.

1 32 kg	**2** 25 mm	**3** 6 mg	**4** 108 m
5 27 g	**6** 3·8 km	**7** 4·2 g	**8** 33 kg

The centimetre

Since the metre is rather large and the mm is rather small we have
another unit of length, the centimetre (cm). Your ruler is marked in
centimetres. Graph paper is ruled in 1 cm squares (over 1 mm
squares).

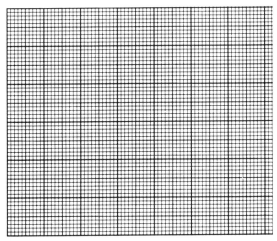

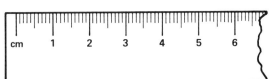

The heavy lines are ruled at 1 cm intervals.

The fine lines are ruled at 1 mm intervals.

1 cm = 10 mm   100 cm = 1 m

Exercise M11

A Change these to millimetres (check on your ruler).

1 5 cm	**2** 8 cm	**3** 4·5 cm	**4** 7·2 cm	**5** 9·8 cm
6 12·0 cm	**7** 14·5 cm	**8** 20·2 cm	**9** 16·6 cm	**10** 30 cm

B Change these to centimetres.

1 60 mm	**2** 100 mm	**3** 18 mm	**4** 27 mm	**5** 32 mm
6 5 m	**7** 14 m	**8** 0·5 m	**9** 2·3 m	**10** 4·05 m

C Which of these measurements are *not* sensible?

1 A man 250 cm tall	**2** An aircraft flying 2000 cm above ground
3 A rope 0·2 cm long	**4** A race of 10 000 cm
5 A wire 100 cm thick	**6** A butterfly 2 cm across its wings

Unit M4 Metric measurement II

The litre

Make a paper box which is 10 cm long, 10 cm high and 10 cm wide. You can make it by cutting out the **plan** as shown. This box would hold exactly 1000 cm³, called a **litre**, of water (or of anything else).

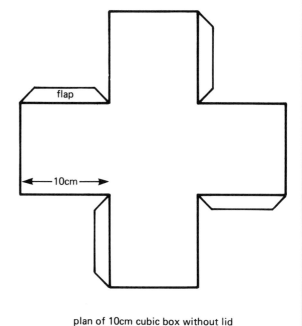

plan of 10cm cubic box without lid

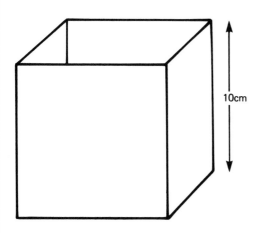

1cm³
to same scale

1 litre = 1000 cubic centimetres

(1 litre = 1000 cm³)

1 litre of water weighs 1 kg

This fact connects measures of length with measures of mass.

Since 1 litre = 1000 cm³ and 1 kg = 1000 g it follows that 1 cm³ of water weighs 1 g.

Exercise M 12

A How many cm³ of water would weigh these amounts?

1 500 g   **2** 1·5 kg   **3** 4·3 kg   **4** 130 g   **5** 100 g

What would these quantities of water weigh? (1 litre = 1000 millilitres or 100 centilitres)

6 2 litres   **7** 500 ml   **8** 20 cl   **9** 400 ml   **10** 3·5 litres

A bath weighs 150 kg. John (45 kg) lets in 300 litres of water. What is the total weight when he gets in the bath?

B Change these to millilitres. (1 litre = 1000 ml, 1 litre = 100 cl, 1 cl = 10 ml)

1 3 litres   **2** 1·5 litres   **3** 0·7 litre

4 0·65 litre   **5** 6 cl   **6** 2·5 cl

C Change these to centilitres.

1 4 litres   **2** 0·5 litre   **3** 1·3 litres

4 400 ml   **5** 1500 ml   **6** 75 ml

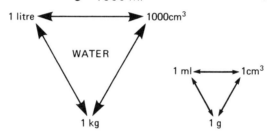

Addition and subtraction of metric units

This is very simple as the units are based on 10.

Always convert so that all units are the same *before* adding or subtracting.

Examples:

(a) 1 kg + 1400 g = 1000 g + 1400 g = 2400 g = 2·4 kg

(b) 12·4 cm + 3 mm + 16 cm = 124 mm + 3 mm + 160 mm = 287 mm *or* 28·7 cm

Exercise M 13

A Add these collections of lengths.

1 4 cm + 11 mm   **2** 2·8 cm + 12 mm   **3** 8·0 cm + 7 mm

4 23·5 cm + 4 mm   **5** 2 m + 35 cm   **6** 4·2 m + 27 cm

7 5·05 m + 10 cm   **8** 6·23 m + 145 cm   **9** 1 m + 25 cm + 1·35 m

10 2·3 m + 30 cm + 145 cm   **11** 22 m + 150 cm + 1·35 m   **12** 6·6 m + 72 cm + 59 cm

B Add these collections of masses (weights).

1 42 g + 550 g   **2** 454 g + 175 g   **3** 1 kg + 300 g

4 2·5 kg + 350 g   **5** 4·2 kg + 800 g   **6** 5·23 kg + 23 g

7 2 kg + 300 g + 1·75 kg   **8** 11 kg + 250 g + 2·06 kg   **9** 1·450 kg + 360 g + 2·7 kg

C Add these collections of liquid quantities.

1 1 litre + 200 cl   **2** 2·5 litres + 400 cl   **3** 0·5 litre + 0·7 litre

4 500 ml + 0·41 litre   **5** 350 ml + 20 cl   **6** 30 cl + 100 ml

7 0·4 litre + 30 cl + 50 ml   **8** 0·05 litre + 24 cl + 35 ml   **9** 0·60 litre + 4·8 cl + 8 ml

Exercise M 14

A Subtract these lengths.

1 1 m − 40 cm   **2** 1 m − 37 cm   **3** 2·30 m − 50 cm

4 1 km − 450 m   **5** 2·3 km − 800 m   **6** 75 km − 8000 m

7 3 cm − 22 mm   **8** 4·5 cm − 10 mm   **9** 22 cm − 15 mm

B Subtract these weights.

1 1 kg − 400 g   **2** 1 kg − 550 g   **3** 1 kg − 320 g

4 2 kg − 1300 g   **5** 3 kg − 1450 g   **6** 5 kg − 2050 g

7 1·3 kg − 750 g   **8** 2·4 kg − 395 g   **9** 0·7 kg − 165 g

C Subtract these quantities.

1 1 litre − 25 cl   **2** 1 litre − 37 cl   **3** 2 litres − 40 cl

4 3 cl − 4 ml   **5** 2·4 cl − 8 ml   **6** 8·5 cl − 45 ml

7 1 litre − 450 ml   **8** 2·3 litres − 520 ml   **9** 4·5 litres − 670 ml

Exercise M 15 (Problems)

1 A 350 mm piece is cut from a length of wood 2 m long. What is the length of the remainder?

2 A key for a lock needs to be 22 mm long. How much is left from a piece of metal 10 cm long when the key is cut?

3 The distance from a school to the railway station is 2·4 km. John walks from home to school (600 m) and then to the railway station. How far has he walked altogether?

4 A rifle has a range of 1500 m. How far out of range is a target which is 1·8 km away?

5 An aircraft flies at a height of 5 km over the top of a mountain 3800 metres high. How high above the mountains is the aircraft?

6 A cake is made from 500 g of flour, 200 g of fat, 200 g of sugar, 200 ml of water and two eggs weighing 80 g each. What is the most you could expect the cake to weigh after baking?

7 A piece of coal weighing 1 kg is burned. The ashes left weigh 135 g. What weight of coal has been used up?

8 Billy weighed 45·8 kg before lunch and 46·15 kg after lunch. How many grams has he gained?

9 A plant absorbs 50 ml of water a day. It is placed in a bowl containing 0·4 litre of water. How many days' supply of water is this?

10 A half litre bottle of whisky is left open. The whisky evaporates at a rate of 10 ml per day. How many days before the whole bottle of whisky has evaporated?

Unit M5   Use of calculator III

$a \times b$ calculations

Your calculator will give you the answer to $a \times b$ if you follow
[C] [a] [×] [b] [∗] where ∗ is +, −, ×, ÷ or =.

A   Multiply these on your calculator.

1 5×4	**2** 3×6	**3** 6×7	**4** 8×8	**5** 4×9
6 3×20	**7** 30×5	**8** 40×8	**9** 9×50	**10** 70×4
11 20×30	**12** 30×50	**13** 40×40	**14** 60×30	**15** 70×70

B   Check the calculations, making a rough guess using first figures only.

Examples:

(a) 42×61 Rough guess $40 \times 60 = 2400$
                        Calculator 2562

(b) 32×18 Rough guess $30 \times 20 = 600$
                        Calculator 576

1 12×23	**2** 21×41	**3** 27×32	**4** 43×58
5 31×31	**6** 42×52	**7** 38×48	**8** 52×60
9 67×72	**10** 71×83	**11** 69×69	**12** 83×84

Rule of zeros

When you multiply two numbers ending in zero, the product must
end in at least two zeros.

Examples:
$20 \times 30 = 600$
$40 \times 80 = 3200$
$20 \times 50 = 1000$ (because 5×2 is involved which produces another zero)

Exercise M17
A   Multiply these on the calculator and check for the correct number of zeros. Predict first.

1 30×30	**2** 60×30	**3** 40×20	**4** 50×80	**5** 40×50
6 40×80	**7** 10×20	**8** 110×430	**9** 160×250	

B   Multiply these on the calculator and check for the correct number of zeros. Make up a rough rule which will help you predict.

1	300 × 20	**2**	40 × 100	**3**	800 × 200	**4**	50 × 200
5	250 × 40	**6**	120 × 1200	**7**	800 × 250	**8**	900 × 700
9	100 × 650	**10**	1000 × 200	**11**	300 × 500	**12**	800 × 1100

Big calculations: The calculator limit

Because the calculator only has a limited number of spaces on the display it cannot show very large numbers directly. It therefore shows them by counting the 0s.

Exercise M18

A   Multiply these on the calculator and note carefully how the calculator gives the answer.

1	40 000 000 × 10	**2**	30 000 000 × 100	**3**	5 000 000 × 1000
4	42 000 000 × 10	**5**	55 000 000 × 100	**6**	670 000 × 1000
7	150 × 200 000	**8**	8000 × 300 000	**9**	40 000 × 50 000

What do you notice about the 'number' part of the answer?

B   The 'operator' has made some errors in these. Can you pick out the errors and put them right without using the machine? Check with the machine when you have finished error spotting.

	$a \times b$	=	
1	30 000 × 20 000	= 6	08
2	200 000 × 12 000	= 2·4	08
3	40 000 × 400 000	= 1·6	10
4	600 000 × 5 000	= 3	08
5	700 000 × 5 000	= 3·5	09
6	1 500 000 × 10 000	= 1·5	10
7	25 000 × 40 000	= 1	09
8	600 000 × 800 000	= 4·8	11

The last column counts the number of tens that are to multiply the previous figure.

6   08 means
6   × 10 × 10 × 10 × 10 × 10 × 10 × 10 × 10

(Your calculator may not be scientific enough to do this.)

Order of calculation

You would expect to get the same answer for 6 × 4 and 4 × 6 because you know that both equal 24. Is it *always* true that the order of multiplication does not affect the result? What about 234 827 and 1 596 382?

Exercise M19

A   Check that these pairs give the same result.

1	235 × 38; 38 × 235	**2**	306 × 279; 279 × 306
3	4561 × 2893; 2893 × 4561	**4**	31 570 × 20 530; 20 530 × 31 570
5	600 000 × 32 615; 32 615 × 600 000	**6**	4853 × 69 696; 69 696 × 4853

B We can also describe this property by saying $a \times b = b \times a$ where a and b are any number you like.

Choose some more pairs for yourself and check that $a \times b = b \times a$ for those you have chosen. Are you convinced that it works for all numbers?

C Look at these diagrams. Each one shows $a \times b = b \times a$ for particular numbers. Write down the numbers in each case.

1

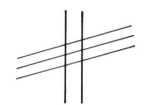

2

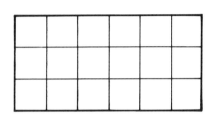

3

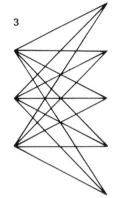

Some problems using multiplication

In each of these problems consider the answer you get from a common-sense point of view. Does the answer seem reasonable? Is the answer too accurate for the question?

Example:

How many minutes have I lived by my twelfth birthday?

$60 \times 24 \times 365 \times 12 = 6\ 307\ 200$ minutes

Exercise M20

1 Take your pulse and find out how many times your heart beats in a minute. From this, work out how many times your heart has beaten in your life.

2 Light travels at 186 000 miles per second. The distance to the nearest star is about 4 light years. One light year is the distance travelled by light in a year. How far away is the nearest star in millions of miles?

3 Suppose a spaceship could travel at 100 000 miles per hour (100 times as fast as Concorde). How long would it take to get to the nearest star? Do you think man will conquer space?

4 If the average wage is £65 per week and there are 10 million workers, how much is earned by the workers in a year? If the government takes 40p from every £1 in tax, how much is taken in tax in a year?

5 Some germs can increase their numbers so as to double in an hour if they are not treated. A colony of 1000 germs grows unchecked. How many are there at the end of 24 hours?

6 To win a cornflakes competition you have to put 10 things in the correct order. The number of possible orders is $1 \times 2 \times 3 \times 4 \times 5 \times 6 \times 7 \times 8 \times 9 \times 10$. How many is this? Do you have much chance of getting the right order by guessing?

Unit M6 Division

Division

Your calculator will give you the answer to any division $a \div b$ if you
follow $\boxed{C}$ $\boxed{a}$ $\boxed{\div}$ $\boxed{b}$ $\boxed{*}$ where $*$ is $+$, $-$, $\times$, $\div$ or $=$.

Exercise M21

A Divide these on your calculator and compare with answers estimated in your head
beforehand.

1 $24 \div 4$		**2** $30 \div 6$		**3** $25 \div 5$		**4** $42 \div 7$		**5** $48 \div 4$	
6 $40 \div 4$		**7** $70 \div 10$		**8** $60 \div 5$		**9** $100 \div 10$		**10** $72 \div 6$	
11 $120 \div 10$		**12** $200 \div 20$		**13** $150 \div 50$		**14** $180 \div 30$		**15** $240 \div 20$	

B Check these by multiplying back.

Example:

$42 \div 6$ $\boxed{C}$ $\boxed{4}$ $\boxed{2}$ $\boxed{\div}$ $\boxed{6}$ $\boxed{=}$ $\boxed{\times}$ $\boxed{6}$ $\boxed{=}$

                           ↑   ↑

                    have a look   *should be*
                                    back at 42

1 $50 \div 10$		**2** $96 \div 12$		**3** $108 \div 9$		**4** $125 \div 5$		**5** $100 \div 25$	
6 $140 \div 20$		**7** $175 \div 25$		**8** $180 \div 15$		**9** $240 \div 16$		**10** $243 \div 27$	

C Find the errors in these answers. You can check by direct division, or by multiplying back.
First look through the questions and see if you can spot the errors without the calculator.

1 $221 \div 17 = 13$	**2** $1650 \div 50 = 33$	**3** $1008 \div 28 = 36$
$384 \div 24 = 16$	$1890 \div 42 = 45$	$612 \div 18 = 34$
$416 \div 8 = 52$	$432 \div 16 = 28$	$1519 \div 31 = 49$
$1936 \div 44 = 44$	$504 \div 36 = 14$	$572 \div 22 = 26$
4 $729 \div 27 = 27$	**5** $5642 \div 62 = 91$	**6** $348 \div 12 = 29$
$1152 \div 64 = 13$	$2618 \div 34 = 77$	$1089 \div 33 = 33$
$1000 \div 25 = 40$	$675 \div 15 = 45$	$4275 \div 57 = 85$
$1440 \div 45 = 32$	$3072 \div 48 = 64$	$2772 \div 66 = 42$

How many did you spot first?

Your calculator will divide any number by any other. It will give the
result as a decimal if the number does not divide exactly.

Examples:

(a) Divide 1 metre (100cm) into 12 equal parts. How long is each part?

C	1	0	0	÷	1	2	=
0	1	10	100	100	1	12	8·3333333

The answer 8·333 333 3 tells you that each part will be 8 cm and 3 mm long and a tiny bit more. (The last three is so tiny that a *million* parts of that length would *together* measure 3 millimetres!)

(b) £25 are divided equally between 16 people. How much does each get?

C	2	5	÷	1	6	=
0	2	25	25	1	16	1·5625

The answer tells you that each person gets £1·56 and £·002 5 or $\frac{1}{4}$p. You cannot pay $\frac{1}{4}$p however as there is no coin small enough.

Exercise M22

A Carry out these divisions on your calculator (check by multiplying back), and write down each answer carefully.

C	a	÷	b	=	×	b	=

↑
check

1	10 ÷ 4	**2**	18 ÷ 5	**3**	25 ÷ 4	**4**	8 ÷ 6
5	17 ÷ 3	**6**	12 ÷ 8	**7**	20 ÷ 9	**8**	24 ÷ 10
9	44 ÷ 9	**10**	45 ÷ 5	**11**	63 ÷ 7	**12**	100 ÷ 9

What do you notice when you multiply back after dividing by 3, 6 or 9?

B Use your calculator to get answers to these problems. Then give sensible answers.

Examples:

(a) Share £2 between seven people
    Calculator   £0·285 714 2
    Sensible   28$\frac{1}{2}$p

(b) Divide a length of cloth 8 metres long into six pieces. How long will each piece be?
    Calculator   1·333 333 3 metres
    Sensible   1·33 metres

1 A family eats 10 lb of potatoes in seven days. They eat the same amount every day. How much do they eat each day?

2 A car travels 220 miles on 6 gallons of petrol. How many miles per gallon is this?

3 An aircraft flies 650 miles in 3 hours. How far does it fly in 1 hour?

4 A man earns £60 a week. How much does this represent per day (7 days in a week)?

5 It costs £130 to make a set of 9 chairs. How much is it for a single chair?

6 Seventeen friends went on a trip to the beach. The outing cost £48. How much did they each have to pay?

The calculator will divide a small number by a larger one. The result
will be a decimal.

Examples:

$2 \div 10 = 0.2$ $3 \div 50 = 0.06$ $12 \div 66 = 0.181\ 818\ 1$

Exercise M23

A Use your calculator to find the results of these divisions.

1 $3 \div 2$	**2** $2 \div 3$	**3** $4 \div 5$	**4** $2 \div 6$	**5** $4 \div 8$
6 $7 \div 10$	**7** $4 \div 10$	**8** $5 \div 9$	**9** $5 \div 8$	**10** $6 \div 9$
11 $8 \div 12$	**12** $9 \div 10$	**13** $5 \div 7$	**14** $7 \div 9$	**15** $6 \div 10$

B Complete this investigation into the result of dividing numbers by 3. Continue until you feel
sure of the pattern.

$1 \div 3 = 0.333\ 333\ 3$
$2 \div 3 = 0.666\ 666\ 6$
$3 \div 3 = 1.000\ 000\ 0$ (Could this be another form of $0.999\ 999\ 9$?)
$4 \div 3 =$
$5 \div 3 =$
$\vdots$

When you are sure of the pattern, *guess* the decimal part of these divisions:

$16 \div 3,\ 17 \div 3,\ 25 \div 3$

Check on the calculator.

C Make a study of the patterns you get when you divide by 8. Start with

$1 \div 8 = 0.125$
$2 \div 8 = 0.250$
etc

D Find the results for these pairs of divisions. Write them down.

1 $3 \div 5$ and $5 \div 3$	**2** $5 \div 10$ and $10 \div 5$	**3** $11 \div 22$ and $22 \div 11$
4 $2 \div 6$ and $6 \div 2$	**5** $6 \div 9$ and $9 \div 6$	**6** $13 \div 27$ and $27 \div 13$
7 $4 \div 7$ and $7 \div 4$	**8** $11 \div 15$ and $15 \div 11$	**9** $14 \div 9$ and $9 \div 14$

Can you see how each pair of results are connected?

(HINT: **Try multiplying them.**)

Unit M7 Factors and multiples

Factors

Fifteen dots can be grouped into 5s and 3s but no other way without
having some dots left over.

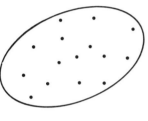

15 dots

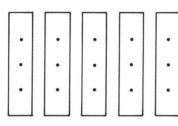

15 dots grouped
into 3s

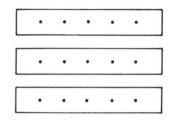

15 dots grouped
into 5s

3 and 5 are **factors** of 15.

Some numbers have a lot of factors, some have just two and some
called **primes**, have no factors at all.

Examples:
10: factors 2 and 5
20: factors 2, 4, 5 and 10
17: no factors

Exercise M24

A   What are the factors of these numbers?

1	14	**2**	18	**3**	24	**4**	22	**5**	28	**6**	30
7	41	**8**	35	**9**	42	**10**	50	**11**	66	**12**	100

B   Which of these numbers are primes (numbers which have no factors)?

1	7	**2**	10	**3**	21	**4**	23	**5**	29	**6**	33
7	43	**8**	50	**9**	49	**10**	55	**11**	59	**12**	73

Factors on the calculator

The calculator tells you very clearly when one whole number is a factor of another. This is explained in the following exercise.

Exercise M25

A   8 is a factor of 24, 7 is not. What do you notice on the display for:

$\boxed{C}\ \boxed{2}\ \boxed{4}\ \boxed{\div}\ \boxed{8}\ \boxed{=}$ and $\boxed{C}\ \boxed{2}\ \boxed{4}\ \boxed{\div}\ \boxed{7}\ \boxed{=}$?

How can you tell from $a \div b$ that b is a factor of a. What happens if b is not a factor of a?

B   Use your calculator to check whether the second number is a factor of the first.

1	84, 12	**2**	108, 27	**3**	373, 27
4	1000, 125	**5**	675, 25	**6**	999, 99
7	1728, 12	**8**	2000, 75	**9**	2548, 26
10	6888, 123	**11**	307 224, 408	**12**	1 822 632, 4568

C   **1**   Do you agree with this statement:
If a and b are two whole numbers, and $a \div b$ has no decimal part, then b is a factor of a?

   2   Is it true that if you find one factor of a number then you can always find another? Explain using the examples:

   (a)   4 is a factor of 100
   (b)   7 is a factor of 56

   3   Go back to question **B**. Find the 'other' factor in each question.

   Example:
   84, 12   12 is one factor
                The other is $84 \div 12 = 7$

D   You probably think factors are very easy. They are, but how can you find the factors of 391 or 1537?

Multiples

Multiples are the 'opposite' of factors. If b is a **factor** of a then a is a **multiple** of b. (Like brother/sister. If Rose is the sister of Jacob, then Jacob is the brother of Rose.)

Example:
$28 \div 7 = 4$ 4, 7 are factors of 28
                28 is a multiple of 4 and 7

Exercise M26

A   Write down a multiple of each of these numbers.

1	10	**2**	15	**3**	22	**4**	32	**5**	50
6	100	**7**	120	**8**	200	**9**	500	**10**	1000

B   Find a multiple of each of these numbers which lies between 100 and 150.

1 10   **2** 15   **3** 24   **4** 30   **5** 16

6 21   **7** 40   **8** 60   **9** 75   **10** 36

C   Find a multiple of each first number which is also a multiple of the second number in the questions below.

Example:

4, 5   Multiples of 4 are 4, 8, 12, 16, 20,
            20 is the first which is also a multiple of 5.

1 3, 4   **2** 5, 6   **3** 6, 10   **4** 8, 12   **5** 10, 20

6 10, 9   **7** 12, 9   **8** 20, 15   **9** 2, 15   **10** 7, 9

11 8, 14   **12** 15, 25

D   You can use your calculator to find multiples.

Example:

Multiples of 5 are found from this sequence,

$\boxed{C}$ $\boxed{5}$ $\boxed{+}$ $\boxed{5}$ $\boxed{+}$ $\boxed{5}$ $\boxed{+}$ ... etc
                    ↓   ↓
                   10   15

Use your calculator to find a multiple of:

1   17 which is also a multiple of 12

2   27 which is also a multiple of 15

3   30 which is also a multiple of 18

4   56 which is also a multiple of 12

Powers

Special multiples are formed when you multiply 1 by the same
number again and again.

Examples:
(a) $1 \times 3 \times 3$, written 3^2, called 3 to the power of 2 = 9
(b) $1 \times 10 \times 10 \times 10$, written 10^3, called 10 to the power of 3 = 1000
(c) $1 \times 5 \times 5 \times 5 \times 5$, written 5^4, called 5 to the power of 4 = 625

Exercise M27

A   Use your calculator to work out these powers. Write down their values.

1 10^4 **2** 6^4 **3** 9^3 **4** 4 to the power of 5

5 2^3 **6** 7^3 **7** 10^5 **8** 3 to the power of 9

9 5^5 **10** 8^4 **11** 12^3 **12** 5 to the power of 7

B   Which is the larger? (Guess first)

   1 2^3 or 3^2 **2** 4^5 or 5^4 **3** 10^6 or 6^{10}

   4 8^5 or 5^8 **5** 4^3 or 3^4 **6** 10^7 or 7^{10}

   7 3^{10} or 10^3 **8** 2^8 or 8^2 **9** 9^7 or 7^9

C   Pick out the pairs of powers from these which have the same value. See if you can spot them without using the calculator.

   Example:

   2^4 and 4^2 because $2^4 = 1 \times \underbrace{2 \times 2} \times \underbrace{2 \times 2}$

   $$\text{and } 4^2 = 1 \times \quad 4 \quad \times \quad 4$$

   1 2^6 **2** 3^4 **3** 5^6 **4** 8^2 **5** 6^8

   6 10^4 **7** 25^3 **8** 100^2 **9** 36^4 **10** 9^2

Squares and cubes

When we raise a number to the power of 2 we say we have **squared** it, e.g. $6 \times 6 = 6^2$ (six squared).

When we raise a number to the power of 3 we say we have **cubed** it, e.g. $6 \times 6 \times 6 = 6^3$ (six cubed).

Exercise M28

A   Write down the squares of all the numbers from 1 to 10 and find their values using the calculator.

B   Write down the cubes of all numbers from 1 to 10 and find their values. Are there any squares which are also cubes?

Summary

Read this summary carefully.

1 a, b and c are three whole numbers and $a \times b = c$.

   a and b are factors of c.

   c is a multiple of a and also a multiple of b.

2 $a \times a = d$, then d is the **square** of a.

3 $b \times b \times b = e$, then e is the **cube** of b.

This calculator sequence will give powers of any number, n.

$\boxed{\text{c}}\ \boxed{n}\ \boxed{\times}\ \boxed{n}\ \boxed{\times}\ \boxed{n}\ \boxed{\times}\ \boxed{n}\ \boxed{\times}$ . . . and so on.

$$\qquad\quad \downarrow \qquad\ \downarrow \qquad\ \downarrow$$
$$\qquad\quad n^2 \qquad n^3 \qquad n^4$$

Unit M8 Standard form

Standard form

A number such as 300 may be written as 3×10^2. This is called the *standard form* of the number. It is made up of (a number less than 10) times (a power of 10).

Exercise M29

A   Write these numbers in standard form.

1 400	**2** 600	**3** 900	**4** 8000	**5** 2000
6 5000	**7** 40 000	**8** 70 000	**9** 90 000	**10** 600 000

B   Write these standard form numbers as ordinary numbers.

1 5×10^2	**2** 6×10^3	**3** 7×10^2	**4** 8×10^3	**5** 4×10^4
6 9×10^4	**7** 5×10^4	**8** 3×10^5	**9** 6×10^5	**10** 5×10^6

We have seen that 200 is 2×10^2 and 300 is 3×10^2. What about 250? This is $2 \cdot 5 \times 10 \times 10$ or $2 \cdot 5 \times 10^2$.

All numbers between 200 and 300 can be written in a similar way. If we use decimals, all numbers can be written in standard form.

Examples:
54: $5 \cdot 4 \times 10^1$ 252: $2 \cdot 52 \times 10^2$ 3700: $3 \cdot 7 \times 10^3$

Exercise M30

A   Write these numbers in standard form.

1 350	**2** 470	**3** 6500	**4** 3800	**5** 75
6 880	**7** 9600	**8** 32 000	**9** 2850	**10** 17 700
11 250 000	**12** 366 000	**13** 48 500	**14** 505 000	**15** 23 700 000

B   Write these standard form numbers out in full.

1 7×10^5	**2** $1 \cdot 4 \times 10^2$	**3** $2 \cdot 8 \times 10^3$	**4** $3 \cdot 6 \times 10^4$
5 $1 \cdot 8 \times 10^3$	**6** $2 \cdot 45 \times 10^3$	**7** $3 \cdot 15 \times 10^4$	**8** $4 \cdot 05 \times 10^4$
9 $5 \cdot 07 \times 10^6$	**10** $6 \cdot 29 \times 10^7$		

C Write this numerical information using standard form.

    1 Mount Everest is just over 29 000 feet high.

    2 The Pacific Ocean has an area of about 64 000 000 square miles.

    3 The population of the USSR is 260 000 000 people.

    4 The 'cow' population of Great Britain in 1975 was 14 700 000.

    5 The number of pupils in school in England and Wales was 8 980 000 in 1976.

    6 The number of cars manufactured in 1982 was 1 330 000.

    7 The number of cycles manufactured in 1982 was 1 830 000.

    8 The number of aircraft operational in 1982 was 340 000.

Comparing large numbers

Standard form is very useful when you want to compare very large numbers.

Example:

Which is larger, 32 48 267 or 456 713.

3 248 267 is about 3 200 000 $= 3 \cdot 2 \times 10^6$

456 713 is about 450 000 $= 4 \cdot 5 \times 10^5$

$3 \cdot 2 \times 10^6$ is between 7 and 8 times larger than 456 713.

NOTE:
1 thousand is 1×10^3
1 million is 1×10^6
A hundred thousand is 1×10^5
A billion (American) is 1×10^9
A billion (British) is 1×10^9 (sometimes 10^{12} is called a billion)
3 million is 3×10^6
4·5 million is $4 \cdot 5 \times 10^6$

Exercise M31

A Use standard forms to decide which of these is larger.

    1 436 517 or 5 236 267   **2** 482 000 000 or 850 000 000

    3 260 000 000 or 360 000 000   **4** 62 913 777 or 62 924 470

B Write these quantities in standard form.

    1 Four hundred thousand   **2** Six hundred and fifty thousand

    3 Three point five million   **4** Seventy-two million

    5 Twenty-six thousand four hundred   **6** Thirty billion (British)

    7 One thousand million   **8** One point four thousand million

C Work out these products on the calculator. How does the calculator handle the large numbers?

1 4853 × 66 295   **2** 5000 × 8000   **3** 50 000 × 8000

4 6582 × 66 835   **5** 5021 × 4007   **6** 9876 × 98 760

7 62 913 × 62 913   **8** 490 000 × 65 000

You will have noticed that when the number is too large for the display, the machine changes to standard form.

Squares

3^2, the square of 3 can be found to be 9 by working out 3×3. The square of any number n is $n \times n$ and can be worked out on the calculator using

   *or* 

Exercise M32

A Work out the squares of these numbers in your head. Check that the calculator gives the same result.

1 2^2 **2** 4^2 **3** 5^2 **4** 7^2 **5** 8^2

6 10^2 **7** 20^2 **8** 30^2 **9** 40^2 **10** 50^2

B Work out these squares on your calculator.

1 14^2 **2** 23^2 **3** 38^2 **4** 42^2 **5** 48^2

6 61^2 **7** 69^2 **8** 77^2 **9** 88^2 **10** 101^2

C **1** Copy and complete this table of squares.

x	1	2	3	4	5	6	7	8	9	10
x^2	1	4	9	16						100

2 Copy and complete this table of squares (use a calculator).

x	21	22	23	24	25	26	27	28	29	30
x^2	441									

What do you notice when you compare this table with the first?

3 The table below shows squares and their differences. Complete the table. What do you notice about the differences?

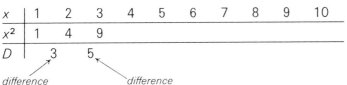

x	1	2	3	4	5	6	7	8	9	10
x^2	1	4	9							
D		3	5							

difference between 4 and 1   *difference between 4 and 9*

Unit M9   Angles

Types of movement

There are only two sorts of movement, going **straight** and **turning**. It is also possible to combine the two.

The letter A is moved about without turning. Such a movement is called a **translation**.

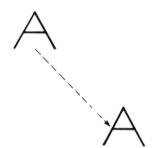

The letter A is moved along *and* turned. When turning takes place an **angle** is formed.

The letter A is turned about various points. Such a movement is called a **rotation**.

Exercise M33

A Which of these diagrams show translation only? Which show rotation only?

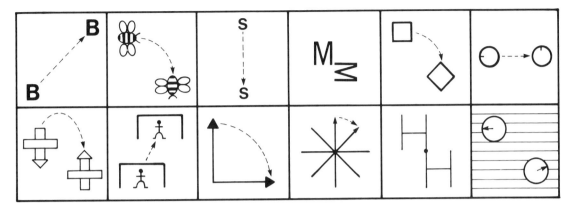

B Rotation and translation take place all around us. For example, when you open a door, or even turn the doorknob, rotation takes place.
List six everyday situations where:

1 translation only takes place

2 rotation only takes place

3 rotation and translation both take place

Measuring angles

The simplest angle to measure is the **complete turn**. This angle is called 360 degrees.

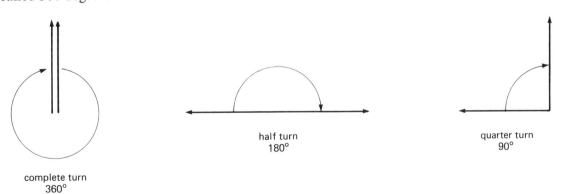

complete turn
360°

half turn
180°

quarter turn
90°

The size of the angle does not depend on where you start.

The minute hand of a clock makes a complete turn every hour. The hour hand makes a complete turn every twelve hours.

Exercise M34

1 John points at the window. He turns slowly until he is pointing at the window again. Through what angle has he turned?

2 Margaret points at the door. She turns slowly until she is pointing at the door again. Through what angle has she turned? Is it the same as the angle through which John turned?

3 The soldier walked to the tree, turned round and walked back again. Through what angle did the soldier turn?

4 Hilary walked to the end of the road and turned right. Through what angle did she turn?

5 Make a diagram for each of the questions **1** to **4**.

Drawing circles

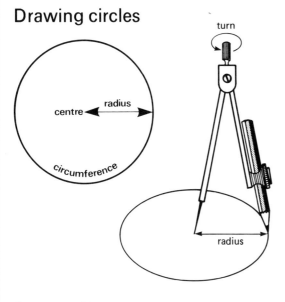

The instrument used for drawing circles is called a **pair of compasses**. The distance from the steel point to the pencil point is the **radius** of the circle. The steel point makes the **centre** of the circle. The pencil point marks out the **circumference** of the circle as the compasses turn.

Exercise M35

A Use compasses to draw circles with radius:

    1 1 cm   **2** 2 cm   **3** 3 cm   **4** 4 cm   **5** 5 cm

B Write about any problems you meet in drawing exact circles. What things do you have to be careful about?

C Practise drawing circles until you feel you are good at it.

Perpendicular

Two lines are perpendicular if there is an angle of 90° between them.

Example:

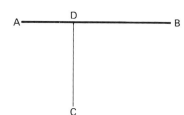

AB is perpendicular to CD.

AB⊥ CD means AB is perpendicular to CD.

Exercise M36

A   Write down two pairs of perpendicular lines for each of the following diagrams.

1

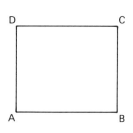

2

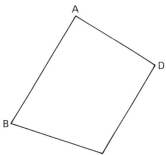

3

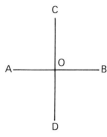

4

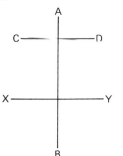

5

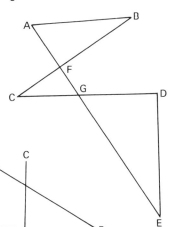

6

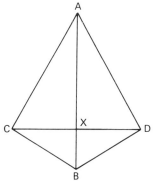

7

B   You will find many perpendicular pairs of lines in your classroom. For example, at each corner of the room three perpendicular lines meet. Make a list of ten different pairs of perpendicular lines.

C   The hands of a clock are perpendicular at 9 o'clock. Find six other times when the hands are exactly perpendicular. (Half-past three won't do!)

The protractor

An instrument called a **protractor** is used for drawing and measuring angles. When measuring an angle take care that the protractor is correctly placed (see below).

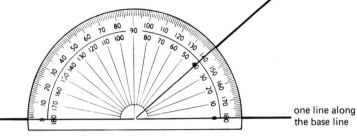

read off the angle from the scale
40° for the small and
140° for the large

one line along the base line

This point is placed over the point where the arms meet

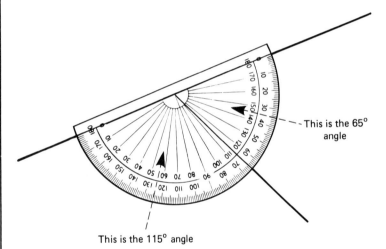

- This is the 65° angle

This is the 115° angle

Exercise M37

A   Measure the angles below with a protractor.

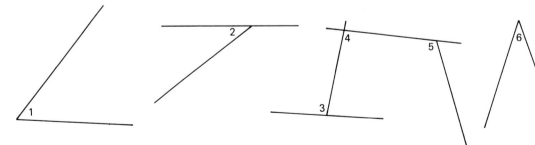

B   Draw pairs of lines which make angles of:

1 10°	**2** 20°	**3** 30°	**4** 45°	**5** 60°	**6** 74°
7 88°	**8** 90°	**9** 115°	**10** 135°	**11** 120°	**12** 150°

C Measure all the angles on this shape.

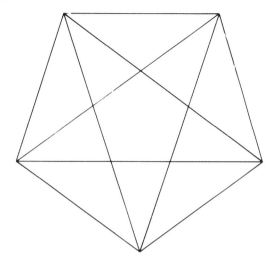

Pie charts

Sometimes information is presented as a pie chart. The angle at the centre of the pie corresponds to the 'share' of the whole pie.

Example:

(b) How Mary spends her day:

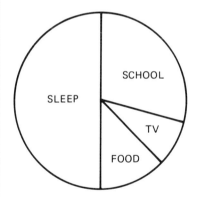

		Use calculator:
Sleep	12 hours	12 hr = 12 ÷ 24 × 360 = 180°
School	7 hours	7 hr = 7 ÷ 24 × 360 = 105°
Eating	2 hours	2 hr = 2 ÷ 24 × 360 = 30°
TV	3 hours	3 hr = 3 ÷ 24 × 360 = 45°
	24 hours	24 hours = 360°

Exercise M38

Make a pie chart for these sets of information.

1 In Newtown there are 200 000 men, 240 000 women and 40 000 children.

2 Paul spends his day like this: sleeping 10 hours, eating 2 hours, football 1 hour, homework 2 hours and school 7 hours.

3 Mrs Keene has £36 a week to buy food. She spends £10 on meat, £8 on vegetables, £4 on milk and the rest on groceries.

4 100 people were asked about pets. 40 liked dogs, 30 liked cats, 12 liked birds and the rest did not like any sort of pet.

Unit M10 Lines

Straight lines and angles at a point

The length of a straight line is measured with a ruler. Take care that
the ruler is placed with zero against one end of the line.

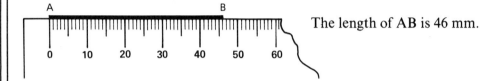

The length of AB is 46 mm.

Exercise M39

A   Measure the lengths of these 25 straight lines as accurately as you can.

B   Draw straight lines of these lengths.

1 AB, 15 mm long	**2** CD, 23 mm long	**3** EF, 36 mm long
4 GH, 40 mm long	**5** IJ, 5 cm long	**6** KL, 9·6 cm long
7 MN, 14·5 cm long	**8** OP, 19·1 cm long	

C   Measure the lengths AB, AC, AD, BC, BD and CD on the shapes below.

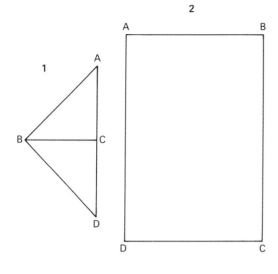

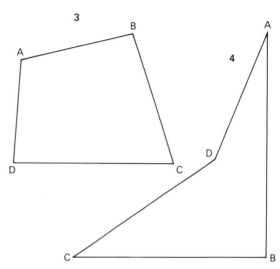

The distance between two points is the length of the shortest line between them. Obviously this is a straight line (unless you are talking about flying around the world or off into space).

A ·   Distance from A to B is 3·8 cm.

          · B

Exercise M40

A   On this map 1 cm corresponds to 30 km of real distance.

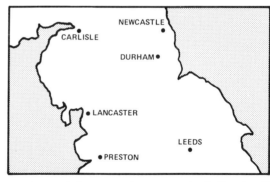

What are the distances on the map and what are the real distances between the following?

1   Newcastle and Carlisle   **2**   Newcastle and Lancaster

3   Newcastle and Durham   **4**   Durham and Preston

5   Preston and Leeds   **6**   Leeds and Lancaster

B   Copy the three points A, B and C on to a piece of paper.

    1   Measure the distances AB, AC and BC.

    2   Find the point X which is halfway between B and C, the point Y which is halfway between A and C and the point Z halfway between A and B.

A
•

•C

B•

3 Measure the distances from X to Y, Y to Z and Z to X. What do you notice?

4 Join AX with a straight line. Do the same for BY and CZ. What do you notice?

C **1** Repeat question **B** but choose the three points A, B and C anywhere you like.

   2 What happens if you choose A, B and C all in a straight line?

D Some of these are impossible. Find out which.

   1 AB = 3 cm; BC = 3 cm; CA = 3 cm.   **2** AB = 5 cm; BC = 2 cm; CA = 2 cm.

   3 AB = 4 cm; BC = 5 cm; CA = 1 cm.   **4** AB = 10 cm; BC = 3 cm; CA = 4 cm.

   5 AB = 7 cm; BC = 10 cm; CA = 2 cm.

E Anyford, Blister and Cope are three towns. The distance by road from Anyford to Blister is 10 km, from Blister to Cope is 3 km and from Cope to Anyford is 4 km. Make a sketch to show the positions of the towns. (See question **D4**.)

F A, B and C are three towns and there is a road between each pair of towns. If you were travelling to all three you could go two different ways:

   A→B→C   *or*   A→C→B

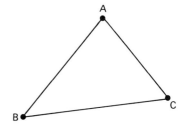

How many ways are there to visit all the towns in the sketches below, starting at A? (All the lines are roads.) Which is the shortest route in each case?

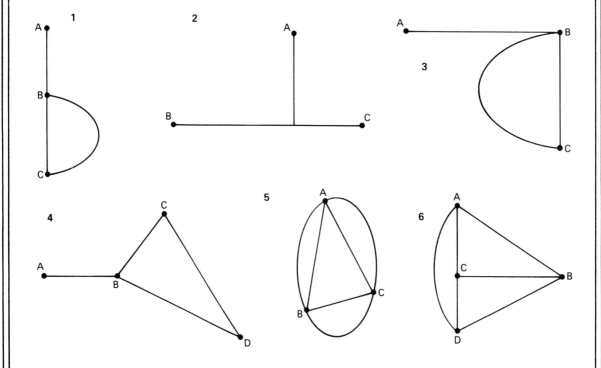

A man walking along AB turns round and
walks back the other way. He turns
through 180°.

The angle on a straight line is 180° at every point (except the ends).

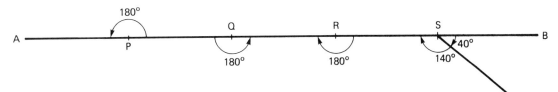

Exercise M41

A   Work out the angle marked ? in these.

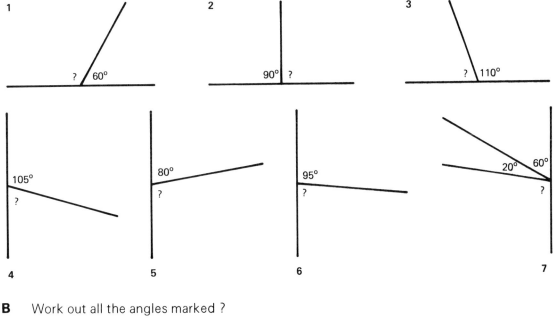

B   Work out all the angles marked ?

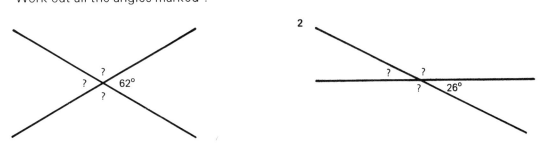

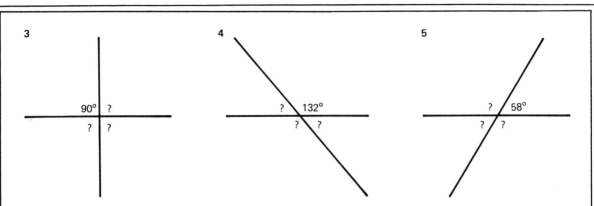

C Which are straight lines in these diagrams? Check by working out the angles and then test with your ruler. (*Remember:* the whole angle at a point is 360°.) Have all the diagrams been drawn accurately?

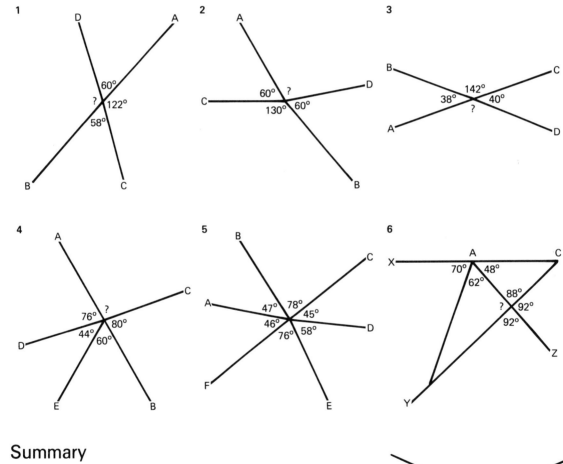

Summary

When a pair of straight lines **intersect** the **opposite** pairs of angles are equal and the pairs of **adjacent** angles add to 180°.

$$a° + b° = 180°$$

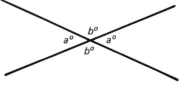

Unit M11   The rectangle

Rectangles

The rectangle is a flat, four-sided shape with four right angles.

Each right angle is marked ⌐.

Exercise M42

A   Measure the sides and angles of these rectangles.

Example:
$\hat{A} = \hat{B} = \hat{C} - \hat{D} = 90°$
Note: Â means the angle at A.

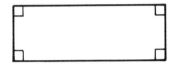

AB = 34 mm
BD = 19 mm
CD = 34 mm
AC = 19 mm

2

3

1

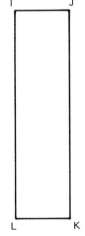

4

5

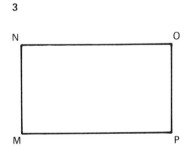

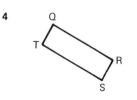

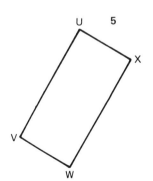

B Measure all the rectangles you can see in each of these diagrams.

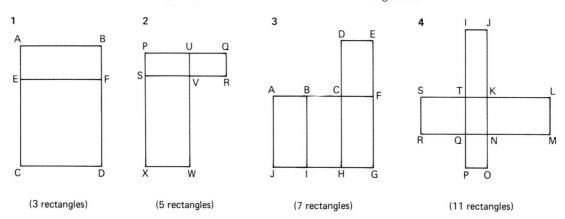

1 (3 rectangles)   2 (5 rectangles)   3 (7 rectangles)   4 (11 rectangles)

C The perimeter of a rectangle is the distance all the way round. Work out the perimeter of all the rectangles in question **A**.

Rectangles about us

Everywhere we look we see man-made rectangles. The reason is that the right angle is easy to make accurately (by folding paper for example) and that rectangles fit together.

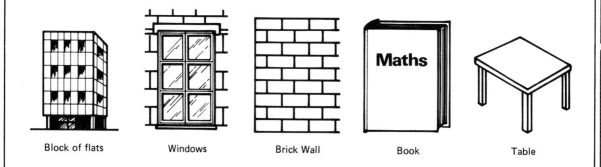

Block of flats   Windows   Brick Wall   Book   Table

Rectangles on squared paper

Millimetre paper is ruled so that you can see millimetre squares and centimetre squares.

Exercise M43 (To be done on mm² graph paper.)

A Draw these rectangles on your graph paper.

    1 Length 3 cm, breadth 2 cm   **2** length 4 cm, breadth 1 cm

    3 length 4 cm, breadth 2·5 cm   **4** length 4·5 cm, breadth 1·5 cm

Which of the four rectangles has the longest **perimeter** (all the way round)?

Which of the four rectangles contains the greatest number of square millimetres (area)?

B   Draw all the rectangles you can think of with a perimeter of 12 cm. Find the number of mm²
in each and make a table which shows how the area changes when you change the longest
side.

Longest side	5 cm	4·5 cm	4 cm	3·5 cm	3 cm
Area	500 mm²				

Example:

If the longest sides are 5 cm the shortest sides
must be 1 cm each.

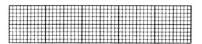

C   **1**   Draw six different rectangles each with an area of exactly 1200 mm².

Example:

This rectangle whose length is 60 mm and
breadth is 20 mm, has area 1200 mm².

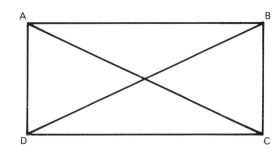

2   Which of your rectangles has the largest perimeter?

3   What is the longest rectangle you could draw which enclosed 1200 mm²?

Diagonals

The lines joining opposite corners of a
rectangle are called diagonals. A
rectangle will have two diagonals, AC
and BD.

Exercise M44

A   Measure the diagonals of these rectangles.

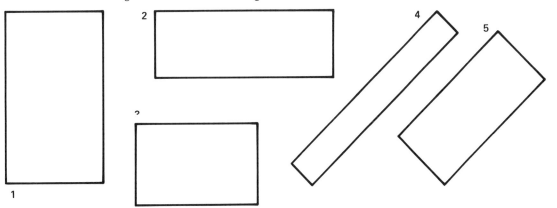

Do you agree with these statements?

1   Every rectangle has equal diagonals.

2   Every four-sided figure with equal diagonals is a rectangle.

B ABCD in the diagram is a rectangle. Diagonals AC, BD meet at O. Measure all the angles and lengths and then list equals, e.g.
AO = OB = ...
AÔB = DÔC = ...

(NOTE: AÔB is a way of writing the angle at O whose sides are AO and OB.)

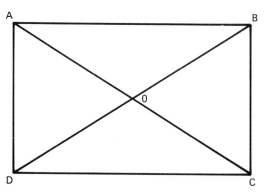

C The point where the diagonals meet is the **centre** of the rectangle.

1 Draw a rectangle, find the centre. Check that the centre is the same distance from all four corners.

2 What shape do you get if you join the four mid-points of the four sides, P, Q, R and S, in the following diagram?

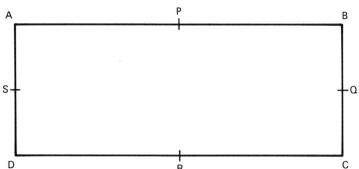

3 Show by measuring that the perimeter of PQRS is equal to the sum of the diagonals of the rectangle. What connection can you find between the area of PQRS and the area of ABCD?

Formulae for rectangles

If the sides of a rectangle are a units and b units then:

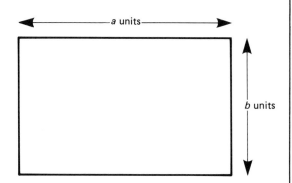

1 The perimeter $P = (a + b) \times 2$ units, $\boxed{a}\ \boxed{+}\ \boxed{b}\ \boxed{\times}\ \boxed{2}\ \boxed{=}$

2 The area $A = a \times b$ units^2, $\boxed{a}\ \boxed{\times}\ \boxed{b}\ \boxed{=}$

Exercise M44a

A Use your calculator (where necessary) to find the perimeter and area of rectangles when:

1 $a = 2$ cm, $b = 3$ cm   **2** $a = 25$ mm, $b = 35$ mm   **3** $a = 31$ mm, $b = 42$ mm

4 $a = 42$ cm, $b = 105$ cm   **5** $a = 36$ cm, $b = 28$ cm   **6** $a = 49$ cm, $b = 77$ cm

B In these examples you are given the perimeter and one side of each rectangle. Calculate the other side and also the area.

Example:

$P = 36$ cm, $a = 5$ cm

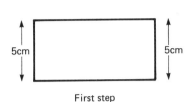

First step

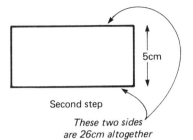

Second step

These two sides are 26cm altogether

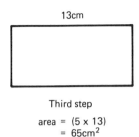

13cm

Third step

area = (5 × 13)
= 65cm²

1 $P = 40$ cm, $a = 2$ cm   **2** $P = 52$ cm, $a = 4$ cm

3 $P = 66$ cm, $a = 13$ cm   **4** $P = 41\cdot4$ mm, $a = 12\cdot3$ mm

5 $P = 695$ m, $a = 380$ m   **6** $P = 162$ m, $a = 69$ m

C In these examples you are given the area and one side of each rectangle. Find the other side of the rectangle and the perimeter.

    1 Area = 42 m², $a = 7$ m   **2** Area = 80 cm², $a = 10$ cm

    3 Area = 140 cm², $a = 35$ cm   **4** Area = 55 cm², $a = 5$ cm

    5 Area = 108 mm², $a = 6$ mm   **6** Area = 240 mm², $a = 12$ mm

Finish this calculator sequence for finding the perimeter:

C A ÷ a ...

The square

A rectangle with all four sides equal is a square.

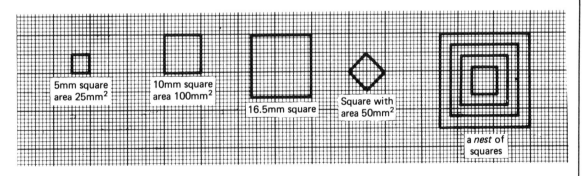

5mm square
area 25mm²

10mm square
area 100mm²

16.5mm square

Square with area 50mm²

a *nest* of squares

Exercise M45

A On mm² graph paper, draw squares with the following dimensions:

    1 sides 5 cm   **2** sides 3·5 cm   **3** diagonals 2 cm

    4 diagonals 3·5 cm   **5** area 4 cm²   **6** area 8 cm²

B Any square is cut into two equal parts by a straight line through its centre. Use this fact to cut out six different shapes whose area is 8 cm². (Think about the best square to start with.)

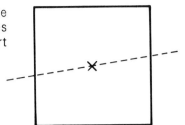

C Cut out a perfect square.

1 How many ways can you fold it over on to itself?

2 Find the centre without measuring.

3 How many 'half-size' squares can you make from your first one?

Summary

Read this carefully.

Rectangle: Four-sided figure with 4 right angles
Opposite sides are equal
Perimeter = $2a + 2b$
Area = $a \times b$ (often written ab)
Diagonals are equal.

Square: Four-sided figure with 4 right angles
All sides equal
Perimeter = $4a$
Area = $a \times a$ (written a^2)
Diagonals are equal
Can be folded on itself in four ways.

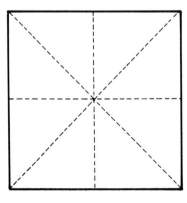

Square showing fold lines

Unit M12 Decimals and place value

Decimals
When you divide numbers you are often left with a remainder. On the calculator this appears in decimal form.

Example:

$16 \div 7 = 2\cdot285\ 714\ 2$

$\underbrace{}$

decimal part of remainder

Exercise M46

A Use a calculator to divide these and write down the answers very carefully.

1 14 ÷ 5	**2** 42 ÷ 8	**3** 17 ÷ 4	**4** 39 ÷ 13	**5** 35 ÷ 3
6 28 ÷ 6	**7** 8 ÷ 10	**8** 33 ÷ 2	**9** 6 ÷ 8	**10** 40 ÷ 9
11 12 ÷ 9	**12** 11 ÷ 7	**13** 23 ÷ 11	**14** 6 ÷ 25	**15** 4 ÷ 11

Make a note of any patterns you see.

B What patterns do you get if you divide different numbers by:

1 3   **2** 6   **3** 9   **4** 5   **5** 25   **6** 8   **7** 10   **8** 11

Try with lots of different numbers and collect up your results.

C Explain what you have to divide by to get these results. Check on the machine.

1 4 ÷ ? = 0·4	**2** 4 ÷ ? = 0·04	**3** 4 ÷ ? = 0·004
4 15 ÷ ? = 1·5	**5** 15 ÷ ? = 0·15	**6** 15 ÷ ? = 0·0015
7 36 ÷ ? = 4	**8** 36 ÷ ? = 0·4	**9** 36 ÷ ? = 0·04

Place value
If you divide £100 between 9 people (using a calculator) each person gets £11·111 111. The ones all have different values although they *look* the same when you write the number.

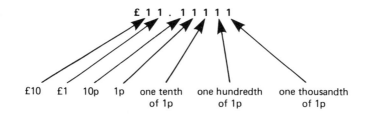

£10 £1 10p 1p one tenth   one hundredth   one thousandth
of 1p   of 1p   of 1p

Each place is worth 10 times as much as its right-hand neighbour.

Each place is only one-tenth the value of its left-hand neighbour.

Exercise M47

A   Which figure shows tenths of a unit in these?

    1 £48·23   **2** £1·04   **3** 3·85 m   **4** 5·55 m

    5 13·2 cm   **6** 11·0 cm   **7** 5·500 kg   **8** 8·050 kg

B   Which figure shows hundredths of a unit in these?

    1 £0·45   **2** £22·60   **3** 4·00 m   **4** 16·65 m

    5 4·05 cm   **6** 100·00 m   **7** 5·450 kg   **8** 2·35 litres

C   The calculator does not usually show any zeros after the last non-zero figure in a decimal.

    Example:
    £2·30 = £2·3

    Leaving off zeros at the very end of a decimal makes no difference to the value. Which of the zeros can be left off the numbers below without making a difference to the value?

    1 £230   **2** 0·450 kg   **3** 0·70 m   **4** 4·0 cm

    5 3600   **6** 0·420 kg   **7** 0450·3   **8** 0·2700

D   Follow these sequences on the calculator.

    1 [C] [0] [·] [3] [5] [0] [=]

    2 [C] [4] [·] [2] [0] [0] [=]

    3 [C] [0] [0] [4] [5] [·] [0] [0] [=]

    4 [C] [3] [2] [0] [·] [0] [4] [0] [=]

E   Which figure shows millimetres in these lengths?

    1 27·056 m   **2** 3·85 cm   **3** 12·345 678 km   **4** 0·362 584 km

    Which figure shows grams in these weights?

    5 45·666 kg   **6** 3·5054 kg   **7** 275 kg   **8** 275·000 kg

Multiplication and division by 10, 100 and 1000

Multiplying 1·23 by 10 on the calculator gives 1·23 × 10 = 12·3.
Similarly, 42·365 × 10 = 423·65. This suggests a rule.

Multiplying by 10 leaves the figures unchanged but moves the
decimal point **one place** to the **right**.

Estimation shows this to be true:

42·365 × 10 = 423·65
     42 × 10 = 420

Exercise M48

A Find the answers to these on the calculator. Check whether the answers agree with the
rule in every case.

1 42·36 × 10	**2** 5·54 × 10	**3** 12·66 × 10
4 2·06 × 10	**5** 0·38 × 10	**6** 0·845 × 10
7 0·104 × 10	**8** 0·082 × 10	**9** 0·0065 × 10

B Explore what happens when you divide these decimals by 10.

1 23·23 ÷ 10	**2** 3·85 ÷ 10	**3** 24·00 ÷ 10	**4** 362·6 ÷ 10
5 27·04 ÷ 10	**6** 6·002 ÷ 10	**7** 0·88 ÷ 10	**8** 0·692 ÷ 10
9 0·056 ÷ 10	**10** 0·007 ÷ 10	**11** 0·076 ÷ 10	**12** 0·0085 ÷ 10

Do you agree with this rule:

Dividing by 10 moves the decimal point **one place** to the **left.**

C Find rules for multiplying and dividing by 100 and 1000.
Use rules to find these and check that your rule gives the same result as the calculator.

1 12·3 × 100	**2** 5·45 × 100	**3** 16·707 × 100
4 27·005 × 100	**5** 3·82 ÷ 100	**6** 145·3 ÷ 100
7 202·04 ÷ 100	**8** 100·65 ÷ 100	**9** 0·32 × 1000
10 0·046 × 1000	**11** 0·45 × 1000	**12** 0·077 ÷ 1000
13 2·5 × 1000	**14** 0·365 × 1000	**15** 42·7 ÷ 1000
16 0·369 ÷ 1000		

Addition and subtraction of decimals

Decimals are added and subtracted exactly as whole numbers. When
adding with a pencil and paper it is wise to write the numbers in a
column with the decimal points in a line.

Examples:

(a) Add $2{\cdot}3 + 31{\cdot}5 + 0{\cdot}73$

                         $2{\cdot}3$ vertical line

                         $31{\cdot}5$ of decimal

    Estimate: $\underline{0{\cdot}73}$ points

    $2 + 31 + 1 = 34$ $\overline{34{\cdot}53}$

Machine sequence: $\boxed{C}\ \boxed{2}\ \boxed{\cdot}\ \boxed{3}\ \boxed{+}\ \boxed{3}\ \boxed{1}\ \boxed{\cdot}\ \boxed{5}\ \boxed{+}\ \boxed{0}\ \boxed{\cdot}\ \boxed{7}\ \boxed{3}\ \boxed{=}$

(b) Subtract $44{\cdot}13 - 27{\cdot}88$ $44{\cdot}13$

    Estimate: $\underline{-\,27{\cdot}88}$

    $(47 - 27 = 20) - 3 = 17$ $\overline{16{\cdot}25}$

Machine sequence: $\boxed{C}\ \boxed{4}\ \boxed{4}\ \boxed{\cdot}\ \boxed{1}\ \boxed{3}\ \boxed{-}\ \boxed{2}\ \boxed{7}\ \boxed{\cdot}\ \boxed{8}\ \boxed{8}\ \boxed{=}$

Exercise M49

A   Add these. Estimate first.

1	$3{\cdot}4 + 4{\cdot}7$	**2**	$12{\cdot}6 + 3{\cdot}8$	**3**	$4{\cdot}52 + 6{\cdot}6$
4	$6{\cdot}04 + 0{\cdot}3$	**5**	$0{\cdot}56 + 1{\cdot}32$	**6**	$0{\cdot}076 + 0{\cdot}48$
7	$4{\cdot}035 + 0{\cdot}22$	**8**	$11{\cdot}28 + 0{\cdot}7$	**9**	$3{\cdot}5 + 4{\cdot}2 + 11{\cdot}1$
10	$14{\cdot}3 + 6{\cdot}5 + 8{\cdot}8$	**11**	$2{\cdot}05 + 36{\cdot}2 + 0{\cdot}75$	**12**	$48{\cdot}2 + 0{\cdot}06 + 13{\cdot}28$

B   Subtract these. Estimate first.

1	$4{\cdot}9 - 2{\cdot}7$	**2**	$21{\cdot}3 - 1{\cdot}9$	**3**	$3{\cdot}04 - 1{\cdot}2$
4	$44{\cdot}2 - 4{\cdot}85$	**5**	$1{\cdot}35 - 0{\cdot}75$	**6**	$1{\cdot}00 - 0{\cdot}25$
7	$0{\cdot}77 - 0{\cdot}38$	**8**	$0{\cdot}95 - 0{\cdot}66$	**9**	$0{\cdot}075 - 0{\cdot}008$
10	$4{\cdot}352 - 1{\cdot}8$	**11**	$62{\cdot}06 - 0{\cdot}85$	**12**	$100{\cdot}0 - 44{\cdot}32$

C   These questions involve decimals and measurements. Make sure the units agree before adding or subtracting.

Example:

$3{\cdot}2$ cm $+ 44$ mm

You can write in cm or mm

cm $3{\cdot}2$ cm $+ 4{\cdot}4$ cm $= 7{\cdot}6$ cm $\rbrace$

mm 32 mm $+ 44$ mm $= 76$ mm equal

1	$2{\cdot}8$ cm $+ 35$ mm	**2**	$14{\cdot}9$ cm $- 0{\cdot}5$ cm	**3**	$3{\cdot}2$ m $+ 45$ cm
4	$0{\cdot}05$ m $- 11$ cm	**5**	$4{\cdot}5$ kg $+ 450$ g	**6**	$0{\cdot}38$ kg $- 0{\cdot}06$ kg
7	$1{\cdot}65$ g $+ 0{\cdot}25$ g	**8**	$4{\cdot}05$ g $- 0{\cdot}77$ g	**9**	$0{\cdot}380$ litre $+ 450$ ml
10	$2{\cdot}56$ litres $- 27$ cl	**11**	$1{\cdot}5$ km $+ 550$ m	**12**	$0{\cdot}87$ km $- 0{\cdot}485$ km

Unit M13   Decimals and index form

Multiplying decimals

It is easy to see that 2×0.4 will be 0.8. This is because
$0.4 + 0.4 = 0.8$.

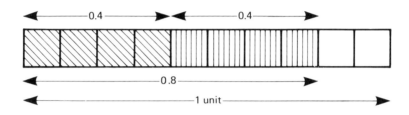

Also $0.5 \times 6 = 3$ because 0.5 is the same as $\frac{1}{2}$ and half of six is three.

Exercise M50

A   Multiply these in your head. Confirm on the calculator.

1 2×0.3	**2** 3×0.2	**3** 4×0.1	**4** 4×0.2
5 6×0.2	**6** 5×0.2	**7** 5×0.3	**8** 6×0.4
9 6×0.6	**10** 2×0.5	**11** 3×0.6	**12** 4×0.8

B   Multiply these in your head. Confirm on the calculator.

1 0.5×4	**2** 0.5×20	**3** 0.5×12	**4** 0.5×3
5 0.5×9	**6** 0.5×7	**7** 0.5×15	**8** 0.5×21
9 0.5×25	**10** 0.5×0.4	**11** 0.5×0.8	**12** 0.5×1.2

When you multiply decimals treat them as whole numbers divided
by tens.

Example:

0.3×0.4 becomes $3 \div 10 \times 4 \div 10$
We leave the tens till last,
$$3 \div 10 \times 4 \div 10 = 3 \times 4 \div 10 \div 10$$
$$= 12 \div 10 \div 10$$
$$= 1.2 \div 10$$
$$= 0.12$$

Exercise M51

A Multiply by these three different methods to check that the methods give the same result.

Method 1: $\boxed{c}\ \boxed{\cdot}\ \boxed{a}\ \boxed{\times}\ \boxed{\cdot}\ \boxed{b}\ \boxed{=}$

Method 2: $\boxed{c}\ \boxed{a}\ \boxed{\div}\ \boxed{1}\ \boxed{0}\ \boxed{\times}\ \boxed{b}\ \boxed{\div}\ \boxed{1}\ \boxed{0}\ \boxed{=}$

Method 3: $\boxed{c}\ \boxed{a}\ \boxed{\times}\ \boxed{b}\ \boxed{\div}\ \boxed{1}\ \boxed{0}\ \boxed{\div}\ \boxed{1}\ \boxed{0}\ \boxed{=}$

Organise your work in the form of a table:

Calculation	Method 1	Method 2	Method 3
1 0.3 × 0.2			
2 0.4 × 0.5			
3 0.3 × 0.3			
4 0.5 × 0.6			
5 0.7 × 0.1			
6 0.8 × 0.2			
7 0.8 × 0.5			
8 0.9 × 0.3			
9 0.6 × 0.6			
10 0.7 × 0.4			
11 0.9 × 0.2			
12 0.8 × 0.7			

B Use method 3 to calculate these without the machine.

Example:

$0.4 \times 0.4 = 4 \times 4 \div 10 \div 10 = 0.16$

1 0.2 × 0.2   **2** 0.5 × 0.3   **3** 0.2 × 0.4   **4** 0.1 × 0.1

5 0.4 × 0.6   **6** 0.5 × 0.5   **7** 0.6 × 0.3   **8** 0.4 × 0.9

9 0.7 × 0.5   **10** 0.3 × 0.8   **11** 0.8 × 0.6   **12** 0.6 × 0.9

Two or more places of decimals

Method 3 works for more places of decimals than just one.

Examples:

(a) 0.15×0.4
$= 15 \div 100 \times 4 \div 10$
$= 15 \times 4 \div 100 \div 10$
$= 60 \div 1000 \longrightarrow$
$= 0.06$

$\boxed{\begin{array}{l} 60 \div 10 = 6 \\ 60 \div 100 = 0.6 \\ 60 \div 1000 = 0.06 \end{array}}$

(b) 0.24×0.35
$= 24 \div 100 \times 35 \div 100$
$= 24 \times 35 \div 100 \div 100$
$= 840 \div 10000$
$= 0.084$

(c) 0.02×0.21
$= 2 \div 100 \times 21 \div 100$
$= 42 \div 10000$
$= 0.0042$

Exercise M52

A Calculate these without the machine and confirm by calculator.

1	0.2 × 0.03	**2**	0.4 × 0.04	**3**	0.02 × 0.05	**4**	0.01 × 0.4
5	0.03 × 0.03	**6**	0.05 × 0.2	**7**	0.25 × 0.2	**8**	0.15 × 0.4
9	0.75 × 0.2	**10**	0.06 × 0.05	**11**	0.06 × 0.5	**12**	0.08 × 0.08

B Calculate these on the machine by two methods.

1	0.24 × 0.6	**2**	0.07 × 0.35	**3**	0.29 × 0.41	**4**	0.43 × 0.55
5	0.62 × 0.98	**6**	0.75 × 0.64	**7**	0.88 × 0.5	**8**	0.09 × 0.32
9	0.54 × 0.65	**10**	0.34 × 0.78	**11**	0.62 × 0.62	**12**	0.89 × 0.98

CHECK: Use the first figure of each decimal, rounding up if the second figure is more than 5.

Example:

(a) 0.62 × 0.72   Check: $0.6 \times 0.7 = 6 \div 10 \times 7 \div 10$
$$= 42 \div 10 \div 10$$
$$= 0.42 \text{ machine result: } 0.4464$$

C Use a single figure check to find the errors in this set of calculations. Give correct answers to all the calculations.

1	0.35 × 0.77 = 0.2695	**2**	0.16 × 0.69 = 0.3104
	0.42 × 0.69 = 0.8898		0.55 × 0.82 = 0.8510
	0.47 × 0.31 = 0.1457		0.67 × 0.33 = 0.2211
	0.08 × 0.44 = 0.3520		0.82 × 0.83 = 0.5806

3 0.82 × 0.07 = 0.0574
0.95 × 0.26 = 0.3470
0.37 × 0.08 = 0.2960
0.79 × 0.12 = 0.9480

Very small numbers

The tail of a decimal represents a very small number or measure. For example, 2.35 cm. The 5 stands for only five tenths of a millimetre. No bigger than a dot.

The following figure shows the importance of the first, second and third decimal place in the number 0.859. The whole circle corresponds to 1.000. You can see that the first non-zero figure in a decimal is the most important.

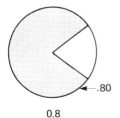

0.8

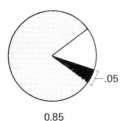

0.85

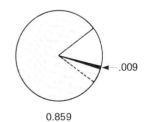

0.859

Standard index form

Small numbers can be written as a number between 1 and 10 times a **negative power** of 10.

Examples:

$0.8 = 8 \times 10^{-1}$ This means you have to divide by 10 once.

$0.04 = 4 \times 10^{-2}$ This means you have to divide by 10 twice.

$0.006 = 6 \times 10^{-3}$ This means you have to divide by 10 three times.

Exercise M53

A   Write these numbers in index form.

1 0.6   **2** 0.9   **3** 0.02   **4** 0.07   **5** 0.18

6 0.25   **7** 0.37   **8** 0.595   **9** 0.622   **10** 0.086

B   Write these numbers in decimal form.

1 3×10^{-2} **2** 4×10^{-3} **3** 6×10^{-1} **4** 9×10^{-2}

5 1.5×10^{-1} **6** 2.4×10^{-2} **7** 3.2×10^{-3} **8** 1.85×10^{-1}

C   The calculator may present very small numbers in index form.* Follow these sequences on your calculator: write down the display as you go.

1 [C] [3] [÷] [1] [0] [÷] [1] [0] [÷] [1] [0] [=]   **2** [C] [5] [÷] [1] [0] [0] [0] [=]

3 [C] [1] [.] [3] [÷] [1] [0] [0] [0] [=]   **4** [C] [.] [4] [÷] [1] [0] [0] [=]

Multiplying mixed numbers

Your calculator will multiply mixed whole numbers and decimals.

Examples:

(a) 13.4×0.3 [C] [1] [3] [.] [4] [×] [.] [3] [=]

Check: $13 \times 0.3 = 13 \times 3 \div 10 = 39 \div 10 = 3.9$

Calculator result: 4.02

(b) 4.85×0.032 [C] [4] [.] [8] [5] [×] [.] [0] [3] [2] [=]

Check: $5 \times 0.03 = 5 \times 3 \div 100 = 15 \div 100 = 0.15$

Calculator result: 0.1552

Exercise M54

A   Multiply these on your calculator. Write out the check for each calculation.

1 4.2×0.38 **2** 6.15×1.16 **3** 0.44×22.6

4 0.32×16 **5** 2.88×40 **6** 3.19×0.04

7 0.06×0.38 **8** 10.81×0.25 **9** 13.24×0.077

10 444.2×0.06 **11** 3.658×1.22 **12** 67×0.0038

* Not all calculators do this.

Unit M14   Fractions and equivalence

Fractions

When one number divides another we have a **fraction** until it is
worked out.

Example:

	3/4	1/2	2/3	3/8	7/10	14/7	15/9
Worked out:	0·75	0·5	0·6666	0·375	0·7	2	1·6666

Some fractions have special names because they are so common, for
example 'a half' or 'three-quarters'. Otherwise they are known as '*a
over b*', e.g.

3/8 is 'three over eight', 4/5 is 'four over five'.

They are also known as '—ths' to show their connection
with dividing up a unit.

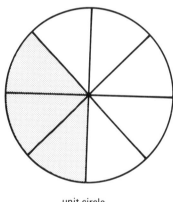

unit circle

This unit circle has been divided equally
into eight parts. Each part is called one-
eighth. The shaded parts make up three-
eighths, 3/8, or 0·375 of the whole unit.

Exercise M55

A   Work out the value of these fractions. Write down your answers.

1	4/5	**2**	5/8	**3**	3/10	**4**	8/10	**5**	6/9	**6**	7/8
7	4/10	**8**	1/2	**9**	3/4	**10**	5/12	**11**	7/10	**12**	8/12
13	12/20	**14**	5/6	**15**	12/10	**16**	18/18	**17**	20/30	**18**	25/75
19	60/30	**20**	8/4	**21**	12/5	**22**	15/25	**23**	16/20	**24**	18/24

B   Draw unit circles and divide each one to show these fractions.

1	one-half	**2**	three-quarters	**3**	two-sixths
4	four-tenths	**5**	two-eighths	**6**	two-thirds

Equivalents

Fractions with the same value are called **equivalent** fractions.

Example:

3/5 and 6/10 are equivalent. Value 0·6

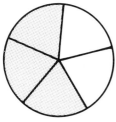 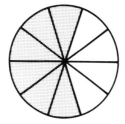

⅗ three fifths = 0.6   6/10 six tenths = 0.6

Exercise M56

A   Find the fraction which is not equivalent to the rest.

    1   4/7, 20/35, 28/49, 44/77, 48/84, 56/96, 68/119

    2   1/2, 2/4, 5/10, 7/16, 9/18, 10/20, 22/44, 36/72

    3   3/5, 6/10, 12/20, 21/35, 35/60, 48/80, 90/150, 105/175

    4   2/9, 6/27, 12/54, 28/126, 70/225, 44/198, 46/207, 66/297

B   For each set of fractions in question **A** find two more which are also equivalent.

C   Find two more fractions which are equivalent to:

1 3/8	**2** 7/10	**3** 9/12	**4** 5/20	**5** 7/15
6 8/10	**7** 15/100	**8** 45/100	**9** 60/100	**10** 75/100

Are they equivalent?

There are three ways of deciding whether two fractions are equivalent.

1   They will have the same value.

    Example:

    2/4 and 5/10 value 0·5 ($a/b = c/d = n$)

2   You can form the second fraction by multiplying the first and second numbers of the first fraction by the same number. ($c = ka, d = kb$)

    Example:

    3/5 and 9/15. The fraction 9/15 is formed by multiplying both first and second numbers of 3/5 by 3.

3 If you multiply the first number of one by the second number of the other you get the same result. ($a/b = c/d$; $ad = bc$)

Example:
3/4 and 9/12

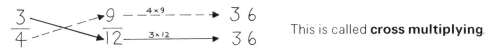

This is called **cross multiplying**.

Exercise M57

A Check that these pairs of fractions are equivalent. Use one of the above rules to decide and then check by the other two rules.

1 3/9 and 1/3   **2** 5/7 and 25/35   **3** 2/10 and 20/100

4 6/15 and 48/120   **5** 11/18 and 99/162   **6** 20/30 and 4/6

7 17/23 and 323/437   **8** 19/45 and 209/495   **9** 2637/1927 and 171 405/125 255

B You can use a calculator sequence to check equivalence.

Examples:

(a) 3/45 and 12/180.

If they are equivalent, $3 \times n = 12$ and $45 \times n = 180$ (Rule 2)

Find n by dividing 12 by 3, and then multiply by 45.

Sequence: C 1 2 ÷ 3 × 4 5 =
            C c ÷ a × b =

(b) 5/9 and 35/63.

If they are equivalent then 5×63 should be equal to 9×35.

Sequence: C 5 × 6 3 ÷ 9 =   (Display *35*)
            C a × c ÷ b =

Use one of the calculator sequences to find the pairs which are not equivalent.

1 3/8 and 453/1208   **2** 4/5 and 276/395

3 7/10 and 623/890   **4** 26/95 and 1430/5225

5 30/270 and 1/9   **6** 485/263 and 13095/7101

Adding and subtracting fractions

You already know how to add some fractions. These are halves and quarters, or fractions where the second number is the same for both fractions.

Examples:
(a)   1/4 + 3/4 = 4/4 = 1
(b)   2/5 + 2/5 = 4/5

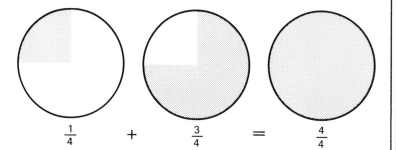

$$\frac{1}{4} \qquad + \qquad \frac{3}{4} \qquad = \qquad \frac{4}{4}$$

Two methods using the calculator

1 Find the value of each fraction then add.

Example:

1/4 + 1/2 = 0·25 + 0·5 = 0·75

2 Read the fractions into the calculator but multiply by the last figure (*d*) before you start.

Example:

1/4 + 1/2 C 2 × 1 ÷ 4 + 1 ÷ 2 =

(*a/b + c/d*)

Exercise M58

A   Write down the answers to these fraction sums.

1	1/4 + 2/4	**2**	3/4 + 1/4	**3**	1/3 + 1/3	**4**	1/3 + 2/3
5	1/5 + 3/5	**6**	2/5 + 2/5	**7**	3/5 + 2/5	**8**	1/6 + 3/6
9	1/6 + 4/6	**10**	2/6 + 2/6	**11**	3/6 + 2/6	**12**	1/8 + 3/8
13	2/8 + 3/8	**14**	2/8 + 1/8	**15**	4/8 + 3/8	**16**	5/8 + 3/8

B   Use a sensible equivalent fraction to work out these.

Example:

1/2 + 1/4 = 2/4 + 1/4 = 3/4 (1/2 is the same as 2/4)

1	1/4 + 1/2	**2**	1/3 + 1/6	**3**	1/4 + 1/8	**4**	1/2 + 1/8	**5**	1/4 + 1/8
6	1/8 + 3/4	**7**	1/5 + 1/10	**8**	1/10 + 3/5	**9**	3/8 + 1/2		

C   Use the calculator rule d × a ÷ b + c ÷ d = to add these fractions. Check by finding the values and adding.

Example:

1/3 + 2/5 C 5 × 1 ÷ 3 + 2 ÷ 5 = (Display 0·733333)

Check: 1/3 + 2/5 = 0·3333 + 0·4 = 0·7333

1	1/2 + 1/3	**2**	1/4 + 1/5	**3**	2/3 + 1/2	**4**	2/4 + 3/8
5	3/10 + 4/10	**6**	1/4 + 3/10	**7**	3/5 + 6/3	**8**	4/9 + 2/3
9	3/11 + 4/15	**10**	7/10 + 9/16	**11**	5/4 + 6/2	**12**	33/42 + 17/7

Unit M15   The isosceles triangle

The rhombus

A figure with four equal sides is called a **rhombus**. You probably
would call it a diamond but rhombus is the mathematical name.

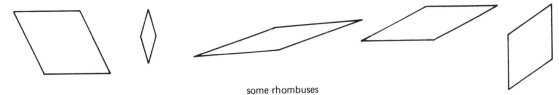

some rhombuses

Exercise M59

A   Find the rhombus in these figures. There may be more than one.

1

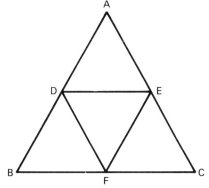

2

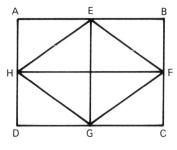

3

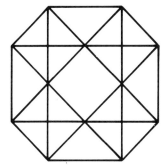

4

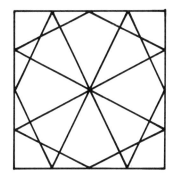

B Follow these instructions to draw four different rhombuses on mm² paper.

1 Draw a line any length under 5 cm.

2 Draw a second line of the same length starting at the same point but in a different direction.

3 Set your compasses to length AB.

4 Compass point at B, draw a part circle towards C.

5 Compass point at C, draw a part circle towards B.

6 Where these two part circles meet is the fourth point D of the **rhombus**.

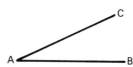

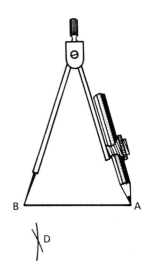

Repeat with different lengths and different directions, three times to get four different rhombuses.

C Measure all four rhombuses very carefully, and make up a table of results.

	Length of sides etc.						Angles			
	AB	AC	BD	CD	AD	BC	A	B	C	D
1										
2										
3										
4										

D Use your rhombuses or your table to decide which of these statements seem true for every rhombus.

1 Opposite sides are equal.

2 Diagonals are equal.

3 · All four angles are equal.

4 Opposite angles are equal.

5 Angle A + angle C = 180°.

6 Angle B + angle D = 180°.

7 The diagonals meet at right angles.

8 The area inside a rhombus is the same as the area inside a square of the same perimeter.

9 The rhombus folds over on to itself exactly in two different ways.

10 The rhombus folds up into a right-angled triangle.

For **9** and **10** you may need to cut out your rhombuses.

Isosceles triangles

When a rhombus is cut in half along a diagonal two **isosceles** triangles are formed.

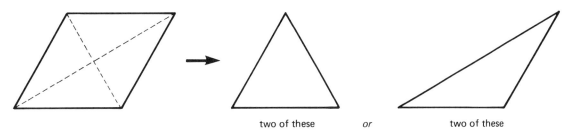

two of these   *or*   two of these

An isosceles triangle has two sides equal in length.

Exercise M60

A   Draw these isosceles triangles accurately. Measure the length of the third side and also measure the three angles. Record your results in a table.

    1   Equal sides 5 cm, angle between 90°

    2   Equal sides 5 cm, angle between 60°

    3   Equal sides 5 cm, angle between 120°

    4   Equal sides 4 cm, angle between 45°

    5   Equal sides 6 cm, angle between 80°

    6   Equal sides 10 cm, angle between 100°

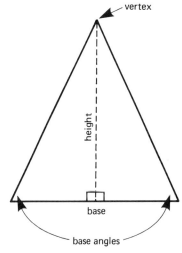

B   Draw the following on mm² paper. Measure all three sides and angles when you have drawn the triangle.

    1   An isosceles triangle whose base is 6 cm and whose height is also 6 cm.

    2   An isosceles triangle whose base is twice its height.

    3   An isosceles triangle whose base is half its height.

    4   An isosceles triangle whose base is 8 cm and whose base angles are both 60°.

    5   An isosceles triangle whose base is 5 cm and whose base angles are both 45°.

    6   An isosceles triangle standing on the base of a square and with its top vertex at the top of the square.

    7   An isosceles triangle whose sides are 9 cm, 9 cm and 4 cm. (HINT: Draw the base first, then think where the vertex will be.)

    8   An isosceles triangle whose equal sides are 8 cm each and whose base angles are 40°. (HINT: Think about the third angle.)

C   Use the drawings you have made to help decide whether the statements about all isosceles triangles seem to be true.

    1   Every isosceles triangle has equal base angles.

    2   Every isosceles triangle will fold up into a right-angled triangle.

3 A line drawn from the vertex to the middle point of the base will make right angles with the base.

4 The area of every isosceles triangle is exactly half of the area of a rectangle with the same base and same height.

5 The line from the vertex to the middle point of the base divides the angle at the vertex into two equal parts.

Symmetry

The isosceles triangle has an axis of symmetry. This means that it can be divided so that its left-hand side exactly matches its right-hand side.

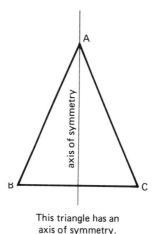

This triangle has an
axis of symmetry.

This triangle does *not* have
an axis of symmetry. The two
halves do not match.

Exercise M61

A Which of these letters has an axis of symmetry? (It need not be vertical!)

ABCDEHMNO

B Discuss the three pictures. Make a list of the symmetries you can see.

C   The figure shows a circle with a triangle. A is the centre of the circle.

    1   What sort of triangle is ABC?

    2   Does the figure have an axis of symmetry? If so, which points would it pass through?

    3   Angle A = 100°. What does this tell you about angles B and C?

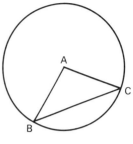

    4   How would you find the exact centre of this circle, using the points A, B, C, D?

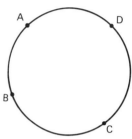

Summary

Read this summary carefully.

Rhombus
Special properties: four equal sides
opposite angles equal
diagonals at right angles
two axes of symmetry

Isosceles triangle
Special properties: half of a rhombus
two sides equal
base angles equal
one axis of symmetry

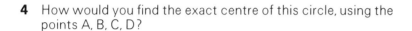

Special isosceles triangles

1   The half square

The angles of this triangle are 90° and 45°.

The 45° angle is very important for making **mitred** joints.

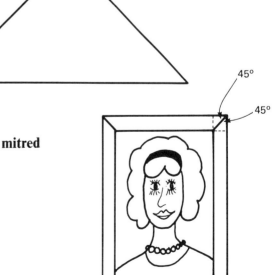

2   The equilateral triangle
Has all three sides equal and all three angles are 60°.

Unit M16 Parallel lines

Parallel lines

Lines going in the same direction are called **parallel**.

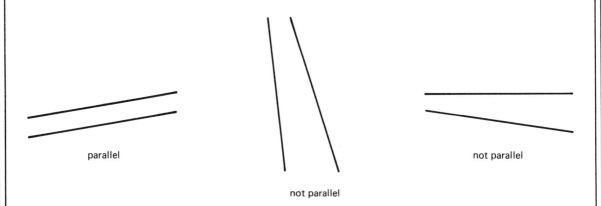

A pair of parallel lines do not meet, even if they are extended as far
as you like.

Exercise M61
A   Which of these lines are parallel?

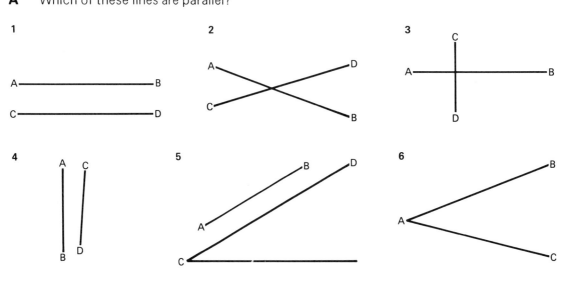

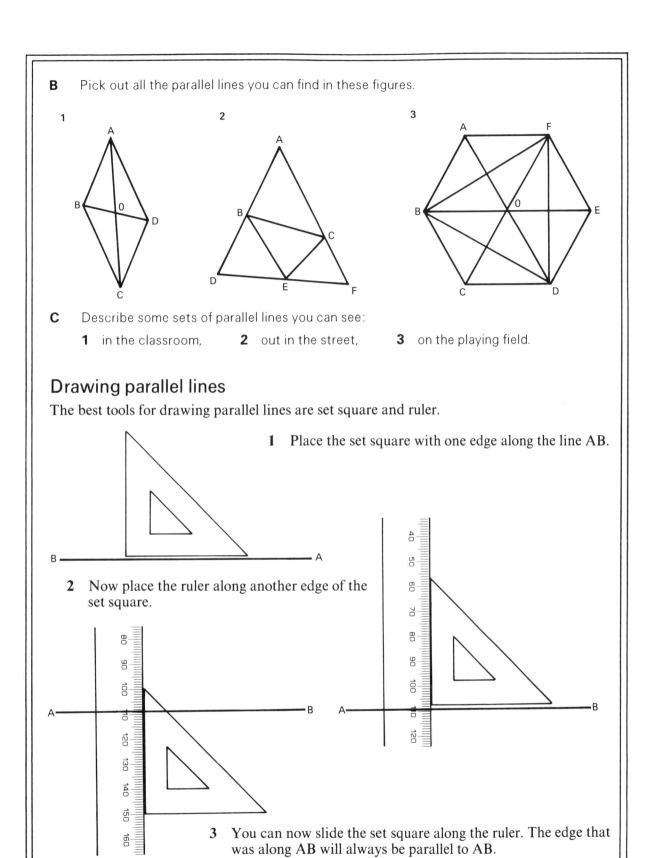

B Pick out all the parallel lines you can find in these figures.

1

2

3

C Describe some sets of parallel lines you can see:
1 in the classroom, **2** out in the street, **3** on the playing field.

Drawing parallel lines

The best tools for drawing parallel lines are set square and ruler.

1 Place the set square with one edge along the line AB.

2 Now place the ruler along another edge of the set square.

3 You can now slide the set square along the ruler. The edge that was along AB will always be parallel to AB.

Exercise M62

You will need a set square, ruler and protractor.

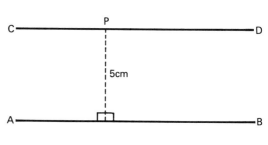

(P is any point on CD)

A Use a set square and ruler to draw these.

1 Draw any line AB. Draw a line parallel to AB and 5 cm away from it. Call this line CD.

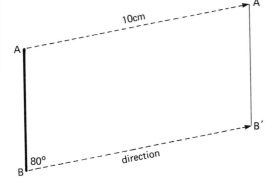

2 Draw a line A'B' which is the result of moving AB 10 cm in a direction that makes an angle of 80° with AB itself.

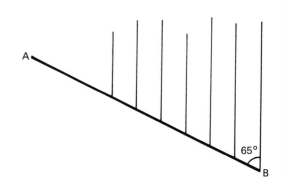

3 Draw six lines all at 65° to AB.

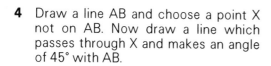

4 Draw a line AB and choose a point X not on AB. Now draw a line which passes through X and makes an angle of 45° with AB.

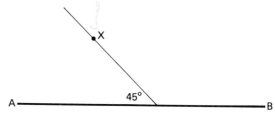

Write a careful explanation of how you drew the solutions to these problems.

Since the lines **AB** and **CD** are parallel they will both make the same angles with a line crossing them. This means we can calculate all the angles in the figure if we know one.

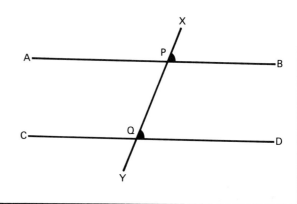

Example:

XP̂B is 70°. What are the other angles in the figure?

AP̂X = 110° (since XP̂B + XP̂A = 180°)   YQ̂D = 110°
BP̂Q = 110°   CQ̂Y = 70°
AP̂Q = 70°   CQ̂P = 110°
PQ̂D = 70°   (same direction)

Exercise M63

A   Find all the angles in each of the figures.

1
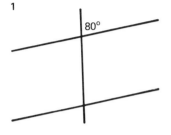
80°

2
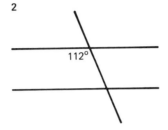
112°

3
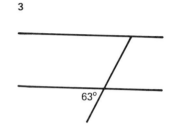
63°

4
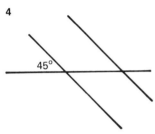
45°

5
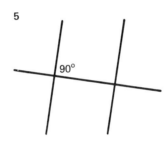
90°

6
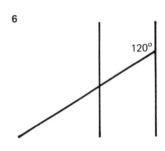
120°

B   Find the value of x in these figures.

1
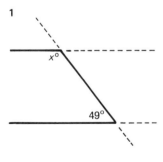
$x°$
49°

2
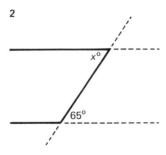
$x°$
65°

3
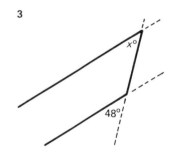
$x°$
48°

4
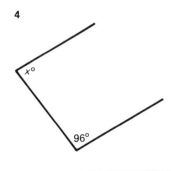
$x°$
96°

5
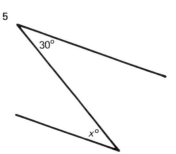
30°
$x°$

6
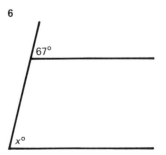
67°
$x°$

C Find the value of *x* and *y* in these figures.

1

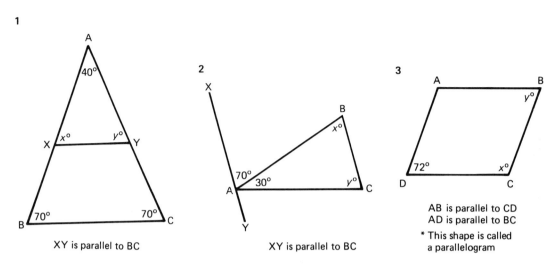

XY is parallel to BC

2

XY is parallel to BC

3

AB is parallel to CD
AD is parallel to BC

* This shape is called
a parallelogram

Parallel lines on graph paper

Graph paper is printed with sets of parallel lines. Many other sets
can be found.

Examples:

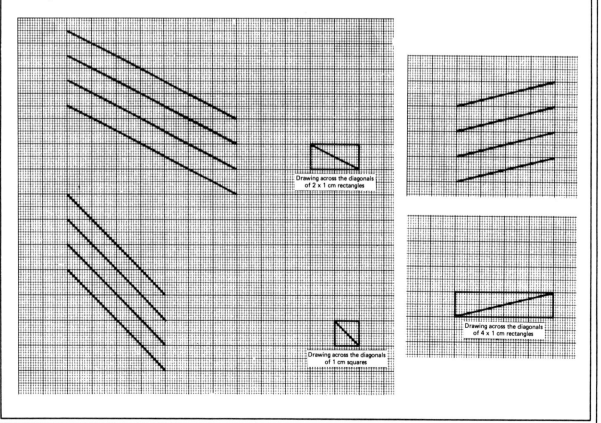

Drawing across the diagonals
of 2 x 1 cm rectangles

Drawing across the diagonals
of 1 cm squares

Drawing across the diagonals
of 4 x 1 cm rectangles

Exercise M64

Work on mm² graph paper.

A   Draw pairs of parallel lines with these properties.

    1   2 cm apart

    2   4·3 cm apart

    3   6 mm apart

    4   making an angle of 60° with the printed lines

    5   making an angle of 45° with the printed lines

    6   making an angle of 45° with the printed lines and two centimetres apart (if you had to jump from one line to the other, the shortest jump would be 2 cm!)

B   **1**   Choose three points anywhere on the graph paper. Call them ABC. Now find three second points A'B'C' by this rule:

       Start at A go 4 cm along to the right and 2 cm up to get to A'.

       Start at B go 4 cm along to the right and 2 cm up to get to B'.

       Start at C go 4 cm along to the right and 2 cm up to get to C'.

       What do you notice about the three lines AA', BB' and CC'?

    2   Starting from the same three points go 5 cm to the right and 3 cm up to find three new points A", B" and C". What do you notice about the three lines AA", BB" and CC"?

    3   Which of these statements are true?

       (a)   AB = A'B'   (b)   AA' = BB'   (c)   AA', BB' and CC' are all parallel.
       (d)   AB = A"B"   (e)   AA" = BB"   (f)   AA", BB" and CC" are all parallel.

    4   List any other parallel lines you can see in the diagram.

    5   Join ABC, to make a shape. Do the same for A'B'C' and A"B"C". What do you notice? (Join ABC, A'B'C' and A"B"C" in different colours.)

Unit M17   Sets, symbols and diagrams

Sets

We often group things together in sets. This can be very useful in mathematics so we use some special signs.

Exercise M65

A   Think about these collections. Explain why it makes sense to group the things into a set. (Look for simple reasons.)

Example:

{Mr Jones, Mrs Jones, Amanda Jones, Henry Jones} Reason for set: All members have the same family name.

1   {cup, saucer, plate, teapot}

2   {apple, pear, plum, orange, banana}

3   {football, cricket, tennis, hockey}

4   {Mary Jones, Fiona Davis, Jackie Green, Julia Matthews}

5   {brown, green, red, blue, yellow}

6   {1, 3, 5, 7, 9, 11}

B   Find the object which is out of place in each of these sets.

1   {egg, sauce, sausage, egg-cup, milk}

2   {tea, coffee, cheese, milk, water, beer}

3   {mauve, blue, purple, puce, yellow}

4   {blue, green, brown, orange, hazel}

5   {postman, miner, cook, secretary, brother, nanny}

6   {1, 3, 4, 9, 16, 25}

7   {triangle, square, rectangle, rhombus}

8   {1/2, 0·5, 4/8, 15/20, 40/80}

Symbols

We use capital letters as the 'family' names of sets and we also use the sign $\in$ which means 'belongs to'.

Examples:

(a) A = {the Adams family}
   = {Mr Adams, Mrs Adams, Paul Adams, Barbara Adams}

It is true that Paul Adams $\in A$.

Paul Adams belongs to the Adams family.

(b) C = {red, blue, green, ...} or {all the colours}
brown $\in C$, because brown is one of the colours and therefore it belongs to the set.

Exercise M66

A   Explain what these pairs of statements mean.

   1 F = {apples, pears, oranges, ...}; lemons $\in F$

   2 T = {trains, cars, aeroplanes, ...}; bicycles $\in T$

   3 A = {3, 6, 9, 12, 15, ...}; $24 \in A$

   4 B = {1/3, 2/3, 3/3, 4/3, 5/3, ...}; $13/3 \in B$

   5 A = {4, 5, 6, 7, ...}; $28 \in A$

   6 P = {▢ ⟋ ▭ ◇, ... }; ▭ $\in P$

B   Decide whether these 'belong to' statements are true or not true. Explain.

   1 $q \in$ {a, b, c, d, ..., z}   **5** $x \in$ {a, e, i, ...}

   2 $25 \in$ {5, 10, 15, ..., 50}   **6**   stop $\in$ {run, cat, dog, win, ...}

   3 $48 \in$ {2, 4, 8, 16, ...}   **7**   Arsenal $\in$ {1st division football clubs}

   4   £56 $\in$ {£5, £10, £15, £20, ...}   **8**   Elizabeth $\in$ {Kings of England}

Diagrams for sets

We usually show a set by putting a boundary around a collection of points.

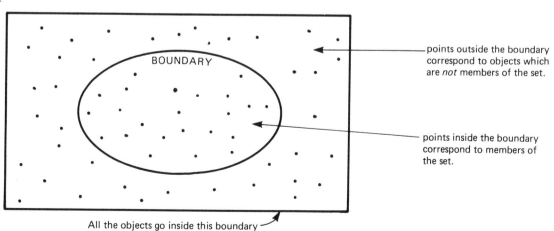

points outside the boundary correspond to objects which are *not* members of the set.

points inside the boundary correspond to members of the set.

All the objects go inside this boundary

The boundary can be any shape as long as it is closed.

Exercise M67

A Make a diagram to show these sets.

 1 The set of letters which look the same upside down (as part of the set of all letters).

 2 The set of letters which look the same in a mirror.

 3 The set of numbers greater than 10 but less than 20.

 4 The set of fruit (as part of the set of foods).

 5 The set of fish (as part of the set of animals).

B Which of these statements are true? (See figure.)

 1 $S = \{b, c, d, g, i, j\}$

 2 $b \in S$

 3 $a \in S$

 4 $h \in S$

 5 $f \in S$

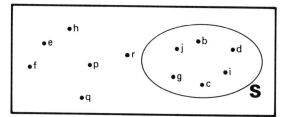

C The following figure is a set diagram for all the children in the class. X is the set of children under 12 years old.

Which of these is true?

 1 Simon $\in X$

 2 Tom $\in X$

 3 Brenda $\in X$

 4 Bert $\in X$

 5 All children whose names begin with J $\in X$

 6 None of the children whose names begin with J $\in X$

 7 None of the children whose names begin with C $\in X$

 8 All of the children in set X are in the class.

Sets of numbers

The idea of a set is helpful when you are working with numbers.
Some sets of numbers are used very often.

Examples:

(a) The hundreds. This is the set $\{100, 200, 300, \ldots\}$
(b) The half, quarter family. This is the set $\{1/2, 1/4, 1/8, 1/16, \ldots\}$ used in measurement.
(c) The set $\{1, 2, 3, 4, \ldots\}$ used for all our counting.

Exercise M68

A Find four more members of each of these sets.

1 {10, 20, 30,...}
2 {2, 4, 6, 8,...}
3 {5, 10, 15, 20,...}
4 {1, 4, 9, 16,...}
5 {1/3, 2/3, 3/3, 4/3,...}
6 {0·3, 0·33, 0·333, 0·3333,...}

B Find out whether the 'loose' number belongs to the set. Give reasons for your answer.

1 {2, 4, 6, 8,...} loose number 149
2 {3, 6, 9, 12, 15,...} loose number 436
3 {2, 4, 8, 16, 32,...} loose number 256
4 {5, 10, 15, 20,...} loose number 1205
5 {1, 3, 5, 7,...} loose number 671
6 {2, 5, 8, 11, 14,...} loose numbers 38 and 502

C $D = \{1/2, 2/3, 3/4, 4/5,...\}$

1 Write down four more numbers of this set.
2 Use your calculator to find the values of these numbers in the set.
3 Is there a number n with value 0·875?
4 Which member of D has the smallest value?

Sets of points and lines

Examples:

(a) a, b, c, d, e, f, g and h are points which belong to AB. The line AB can be looked on as **a set of points**.

(b) p, q, r, s, t, u, v are points inside the square ABCD. They belong to the set of points that makes up the space inside the square.

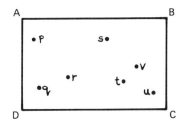

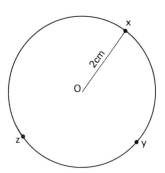

(c) x, y and z are three of the points which are 2 cm from O. The complete set of points 2 cm from O consists of the circle.

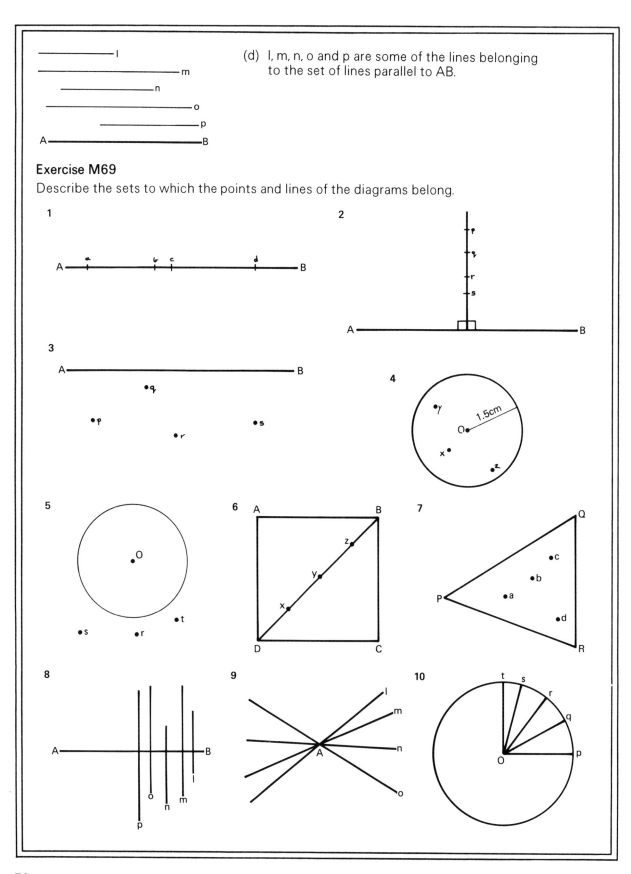

(d) l, m, n, o and p are some of the lines belonging
to the set of lines parallel to AB.

Exercise M69

Describe the sets to which the points and lines of the diagrams belong.

1

2

3

4

5

6

7

8

9

10

Unit M18   Mapping

Mapping

When two sets are connected, member for member, we say set *A*
maps on to set *B*.

Example:
{A, B, C, D, E ...}   and   {a, b, c, d, e ...}
The capital letters map on to the small letters.

We can show the connection by arrows.

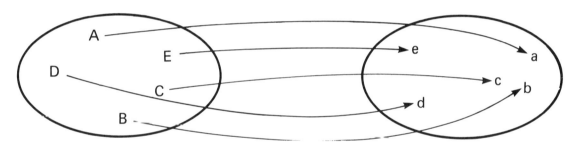

Exercise M70

A   Copy these words and diagrams. Show by arrows how the words map on to the diagrams.

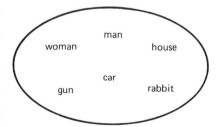

B   Map these sets of shapes on to the set {1, 2, 3, 4, 5}. Explain how you do it.

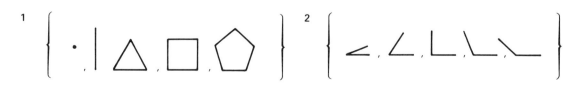

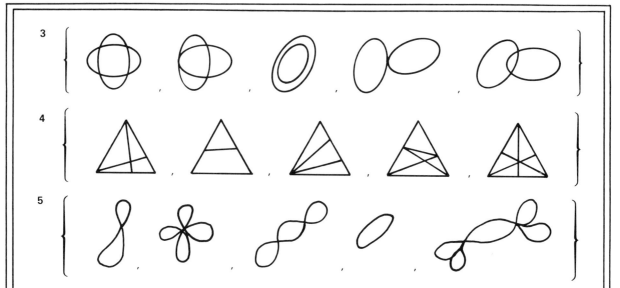

Mapping on to numbers

Whenever we measure objects or put them in order we are mapping on to numbers.

Examples:

jockeys and horses are numbered

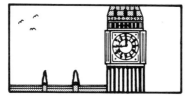

the hours of the day are numbered

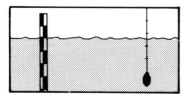

the depth of the sea is measured by numbers

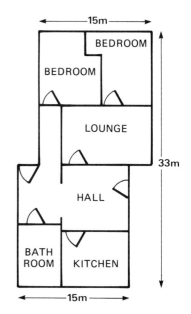

Exercise M71

A What mapping is taking place in these situations?

  1 Kilogram packets of sugar are sold in a shop at 45p per kg.

  2 Wood is sold at 26p a metre.

  3 A thermometer measures the temperature every hour.

  4 A spring is stretched by hanging weights on it.

  5 The plan of a house is marked with lengths and rooms.

Approximating

If we only want a whole number answer, then we map the result of
the calculation on to the nearest whole number.

Examples: $1·4 + 2·3 = 3·7 \rightarrow 4$ $2·07 \times 5·85 = 12·1095 \rightarrow 12$ $5·6 \times 2·8 = 15·68 \rightarrow 16$

B Map these calculations on to the whole number answers.

1 $3·2 \times 4·5$	**2** $3·7 + 6·6$	**3** $4·1 \times 1·03$
4 $2·6 - 1·75$	**5** $13·2 \div 17$	**6** $49 \times 4·9$
7 $66 - 4·5$	**8** $8·5 \times 3·3$	**9** $7 \div 9$

C If we only want a result correct to one decimal place, we map our answers on to the set $\{0·1, 0·2,\ldots, 1·0, 1·1,\ldots, 2·0,\ldots\}$.

Map these calculations on to numbers correct to one decimal place.

1 $0·4 \times 1·6$	**2** $3·2 \times 1·8$	**3** $0·3 + 0·5$
4 $0·6 \times 0·8$	**5** $23 \times 1·6$	**6** $5·3 \div 16$
7 $2·85 - 0·42$	**8** $4·07 - 0·03$	**9** $15 \div 200$

Mapping on to the number line

1 Start with a pair of number lines. (Two rulers or lines drawn on strips of graph paper)

2 Move L_2 so that the zero comes exactly below 4.

$\{4, 5, 6, 7, \ldots\} \rightarrow \{0, 1, 2, 3 \ldots\}$ and every number on L_1 maps on to
a number 4 less than itself on L_2.

We write this: $n \rightarrow n - 4$

Clearly 4 maps on to zero,

3 maps on to the number 1 less than zero (-1),

2 maps on to the number 2 less than zero (-2),

1 maps on to the number 3 less than zero (-3),

0 maps on to the number 4 less than zero (-4).

Exercise M72

A Describe the mappings which arise from moving L_2 in the following ways. Write the mapping as $n \rightarrow \ldots$ Say what happens to $\{0, 1, 2, 3, \ldots\}$ in each case.

1

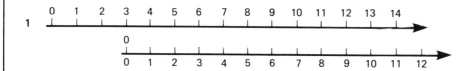

2

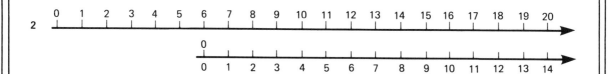

3

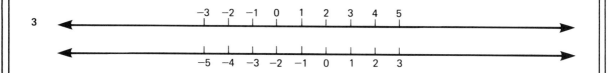

4

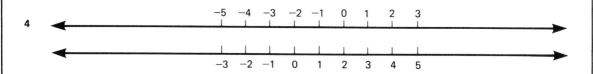

B Draw lines to show these mappings. Find the result of mapping $-5, -3, -2, -1, 0, 1, 2$ and 3 in each case.

1 $n \rightarrow n - 3$ **2** $n \rightarrow n - 6$ **3** $n \rightarrow n + 2$ **4** $n \rightarrow n + 5$

C

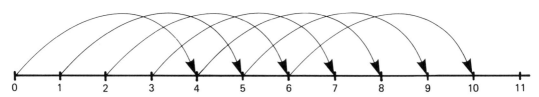

The figure shows the mapping $n \rightarrow n + 4$ on a single line. Show these mappings on a single line.

1 $n \rightarrow n + 2$ **2** $n \rightarrow n - 3$ **3** $n \rightarrow n + 10$

4 $n \rightarrow n - 6$ **5** $n \rightarrow n + n$ **6** $n \rightarrow n + \frac{1}{2}n$

Unit M19   Problem Solving I

Problem solving

Problem solving starts with looking at information. First you take a
main impression, then look in more detail. Finally you take and
record measurement.

Example:

Main impression: A large room with a stage and seats.

More detail: A gallery, the American flag, glass eagle in the ceiling, portrait of presidents.

Measurement: It is possible to count the number of seats and estimate the number of people the
room would hold. The size of the room can also be estimated.

Exercise M73

A   Look at each of these pictures. Write down what you first notice. Then write in more detail. Finally measure some things you feel to be important.

B   Treat each of these diagrams in the same way as the photographs in A.

1

2

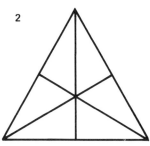

3

4

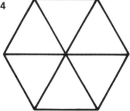

C Write down all the information you can find out from these diagrams.

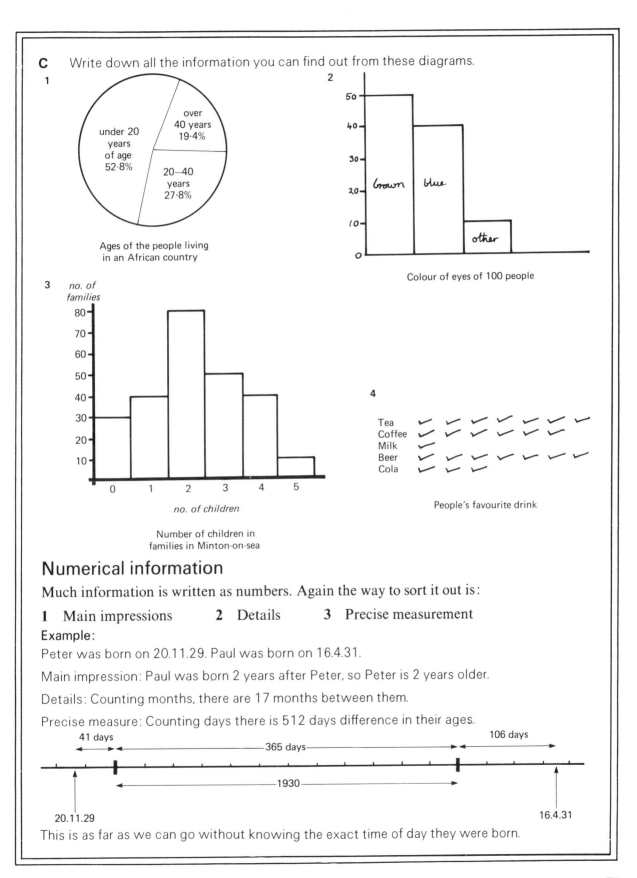

1

over
40 years
19·4%

under 20
years
of age
52·8%

20—40
years
27·8%

Ages of the people living
in an African country

2

Colour of eyes of 100 people

3 *no. of families*

no. of children

Number of children in
families in Minton-on-sea

4

Tea
Coffee
Milk
Beer
Cola

People's favourite drink

Numerical information

Much information is written as numbers. Again the way to sort it out is:

1 Main impressions   **2** Details   **3** Precise measurement

Example:

Peter was born on 20.11.29. Paul was born on 16.4.31.

Main impression: Paul was born 2 years after Peter, so Peter is 2 years older.

Details: Counting months, there are 17 months between them.

Precise measure: Counting days there is 512 days difference in their ages.

41 days   ◄———— 365 days ————►   106 days

◄————— 1930 —————►

20.11.29   16.4.31

This is as far as we can go without knowing the exact time of day they were born.

79

Exercise M74

A Find out all you can from these sets of information.

   1 Janet was born on 13.6.67. Mary was born on 22.3.65.

   2 A motor bike can be bought for £12 per month for 3 years, for £17 per month for two years or for £320 cash.

   3 A playing field is 142·6 metres long and 77·5 metres wide.

   4 Return air tickets can be bought to Paris £28 (215 miles), to Rome £130 (908 miles), to Athens £160 (1500 miles), to Istanbul £207 (1562 miles), to Jerusalem £170 (2000 miles), to New York £110 (3440 miles).

B Find out as much as you can from the information below.

   1 Populations and areas of some countries.

	Area in square miles	Population in thousands (1969)
Japan	142 719	102 320
Italy	116 286	53 170
United Kingdom	94 500	55 530
USA	3 615 212	203 220
Australia	2 967 909	12 300

   2 Some facts about the earth.

   Age of the earth: at least 4500 million years

   Area of surface: 196 950 000 square miles

   Land surface: 57 510 000 square miles

   Equatorial circumference: 24 902 miles

   Meridional circumference: 24 860 miles

   Mass: 6 586 000 000 000 000 000 000 tons

   The earth makes a complete journey around the sun every 365 days 5 hours 48 minutes 46 secs.

   The earth makes a complete rotation on its axis in 23 hours 56 minutes.

   The earth travels round the sun at 66 000 miles per hour.

   3 The oceans of the earth.

	Area (sq km)	Average depth (m)	Greatest depth (m)
Pacific	163 million	4320	11 138
Atlantic	80·6 million	3963	9275
Indian	72·5 million	4000	7067
Arctic	14·1 million	1290	5492
Britain (comparison)	0·25 million	55 (North Sea)	1360 (height of Ben Nevis)

80

Unit M20 Symmetry

Symmetry

If you put a blob of paint onto a piece of paper and then fold and press it you make a picture with an axis of **symmetry**.

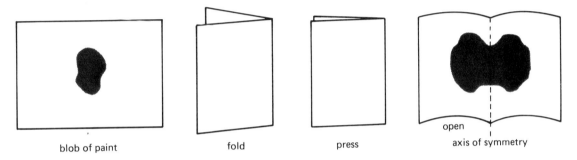

blob of paint   fold   press   axis of symmetry

Similar objects and patterns can be made by folding and cutting paper.

Exercise M75

You will need paper, scissors, ruler and pencil.

A   Take a piece of paper and fold it once. Find what shapes you make when you cut as shown along the dotted lines.

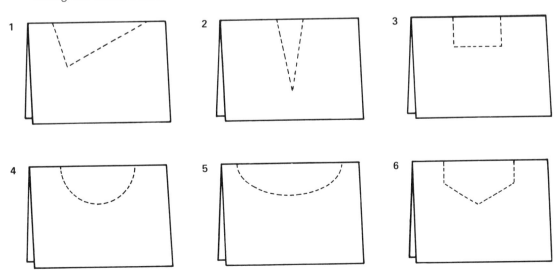

B Fold and cut to make these shapes.

1 rectangle   **2** square   **3** isosceles triangle

4 rhombus   **5** equilateral triangle   **6** 45° right-angled triangle (half-square)

C Fold a piece of paper twice. Find what shapes you get when you cut as shown along the dotted lines. Guess what the shape will look like before you cut it out.

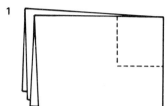 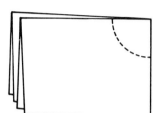 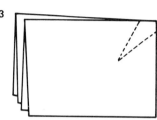

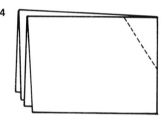 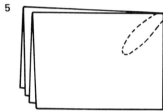 

D Use double fold, corner cutting to cut out these (on mm² graph paper).

1 A square, sides 3 cm   **2** A square whose area is 2 cm²

3 A cross whose area is 12 cm²   **4** A circle

5 A rectangle   **6** A four-pointed star

Axis of symmetry

When a figure has an axis of symmetry we can spot a lot of geometry.

Example:

Every isosceles triangle ABC has an axis of symmetry. A fold along AX would:

1 fold B on to C,

2 fold AB on to AC,

3 fold BX on to XC,

4 fold BX̂A on to CX̂A,

5 fold BÂX on to XÂC.

We can therefore say:

1 $\hat{B} = \hat{C}$ **2** BX = CX

3 BX̂A = CX̂A = 90°   **4** BÂX = CÂX

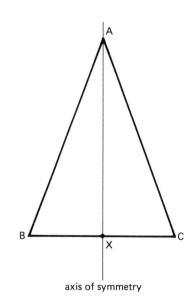

axis of symmetry

Exercise M76

A Copy these figures carefully and mark in an axis of symmetry for each one.

1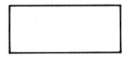

2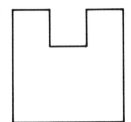

3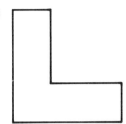

4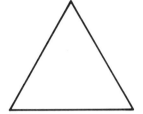

5

6

7

8

B **1** The figure ABCD has an axis of symmetry XY. Write down all the equal lengths and angles on the figure that result.

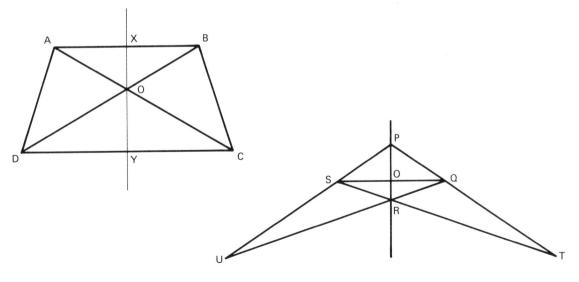

2 The figure PQRS also has an axis of symmetry. Write down all this tells you about the whole figure.

83

C   The line XOA is an axis of symmetry for the figure. Use this fact to find:

1   a length equal to BX

2   a length equal to OB

3   a length equal to AB

4   an angle equal to OB̂X

5   an angle equal to OX̂B

6   an angle equal to OB̂A

7   an angle equal to BÔX

8   an angle equal to 90°

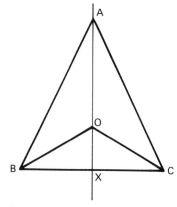

Point symmetry

A shape that can be turned to fit over itself has point symmetry. (We do not count turning through 360°.) The point symmetry of a shape can be checked with a drawing pin and tracing paper.

Example:

1   Cover XY with tracing paper. Copy the line and the point O.

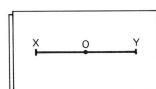

2   Put the drawing pin through both pieces of paper and turn the tracing paper.

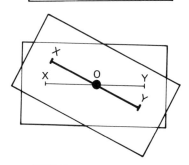

3   When the trace has turned through 180° the line XY will be covered by its image.

Exercise M77

You will need tracing paper, ruler and drawing pin.

A   Find which of these shapes has a point of symmetry.

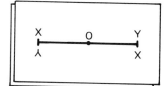

1

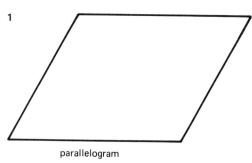

parallelogram

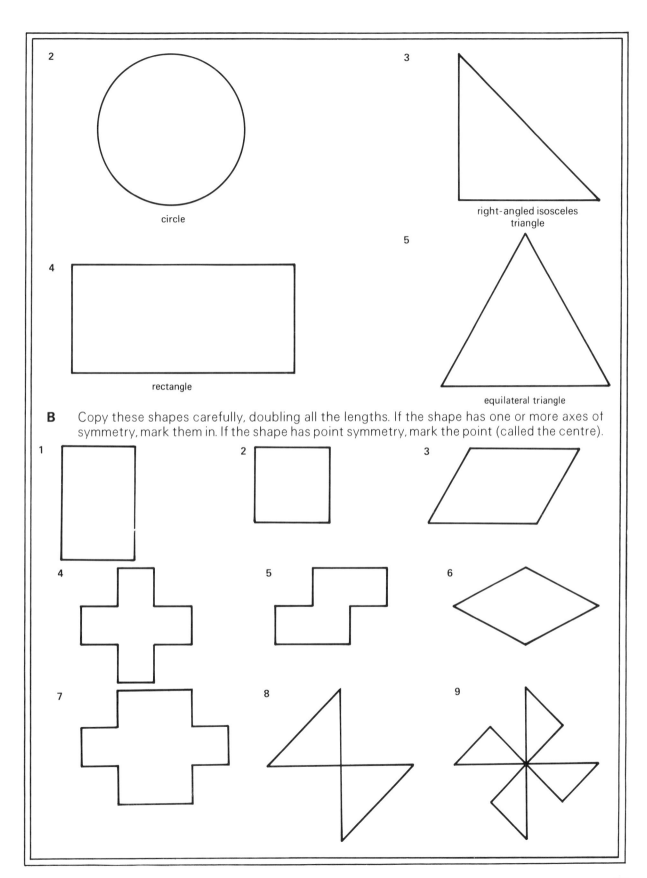

2

circle

3

right-angled isosceles triangle

5

4

rectangle

equilateral triangle

B Copy these shapes carefully, doubling all the lengths. If the shape has one or more axes of symmetry, mark them in. If the shape has point symmetry, mark the point (called the centre).

1

2

3

4

5

6

7

8

9

Number symmetry

Some words read the same backwards and forwards. Level, for example. Can you think of any others? There are not many words like this, but there are plenty of numbers. 11, 22, 33, . . ., 101, 454, 4664.

Sets of numbers can have symmetry.

Example:

{1, 3, 5, 7, 9}

3 is 2 less than 5, 7 is 2 more than 5
1 is 4 less than 5, 9 is 4 more than 5

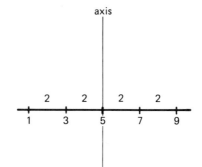

Exercise M78

A   Find symmetrical numbers with these properties.

   1   The digits add up to 4

   2   The digits multiply to 9

   3   The number is also a square number ($n \times n$)

   4   The number is a multiple of 8

   5   The digits add up to 2 and multiply to 0

   6   The number is also a cube ($n \times n \times n$)

B   Which of these sets of numbers are symmetrical. Give your reasons.

   1   {2, 4, 6, 8, 10}   **2**   {1, 3, 5, 7, 9, 11}   **3**   {16, 18, 20, 22}

   4   {2, 4, 8}   **5**   {3, 6, 9, 12}   **6**   {7, 8, 10, 12, 14}

   7   {1, 3, 9, 27}   **8**   {10, 100, 1000}   **9**   {4·1, 4·2, 4·3, 4·4, 4·5}

C   Make dot patterns for all the numbers up to 10. For each number make a pattern with at least one axis of symmetry and point symmetry.

   Example:

   5 has point symmetry and four axes of symmetry.

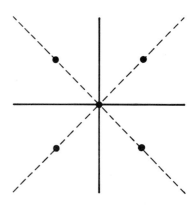

Unit M21 Graphs and co-ordinates

An address in space

Every point can be given an 'address' by using a pair of straight lines at right angles. The lines are marked as shown.

The line from left to right is the x **axis**.

The line from bottom to top is the y **axis**.

The point A is given the address (4, 2). This stands for 4 units in the x direction and 2 units in the y direction.

The pair of numbers (4, 2) are called the **co-ordinates** of the point.

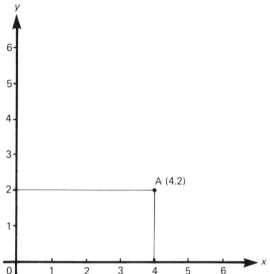

Exercise M79

A Write down the co-ordinates of the points A, B, C, D, E, etc.

B Find the points which correspond to these co-ordinates. What words are made by the letters?

1 (7, 4); (0, 4); (7, 2)

2 (6, 5); (0, 4); (2, 6)

3 (1, 1); (3, 1); (4, 3); (2, 2); (3, 5)

4 (3, 5); (6, 5); (4, 3); (1, 1); (4, 0)

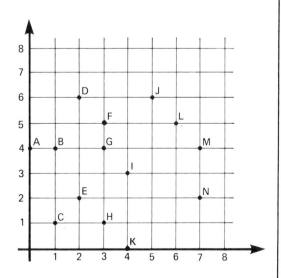

C   For the point (7, 4), the 7 is the *x* **co-ordinate**, and the 4 is the *y* **co-ordinate**

1   What are the *x* co-ordinates of the points F, G, H?

2   What are the *y* co-ordinates of the points A, B, G and M?

3   What can you say about points having the same *x* co-ordinate?

4   What can you say about points having the same *y* co-ordinate?

Sets of points and their co-ordinates

When you look carefully at the co-ordinates of a set of points, you can obtain information about the points themselves.

Example:

If points A, B, C, D, E have co-ordinates
(0, 4); (1, 4); (3, 4); (5, 4); (6, 4), what
can you say about the points?

   All five points have the same *y* co-ordinate. So they will all be found on a line parallel to the *x* axis.

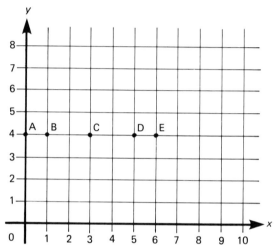

Exercise M80

A   Look carefully at these co-ordinates. Try to guess where the points would be and how they are connected. Then draw *x* and *y* axes and mark in the points.

1   P (1, 1); Q (2, 2); R (3, 3); S (4, 4).   2   W (3, 2); X (3, 4); Y (3, 6); Z (3, 7).

3   K (1, 4); L (2, 4); M (4, 4); N (5, 4).

4   A (1, 3); B (2, 4); C (3, 5); D (4, 6).

B   1   Write down the co-ordinates for all the points on each of the lines. What do you notice about the pairs of numbers?

2   The sets of points IBR, JCS and KDT all lie on straight lines. How does this show in their co-ordinates? (Write down the co-ordinates and look for a pattern.)

3   A line is drawn joining (0, 7) and (7, 0). Make a list of the co-ordinates and some of the points which lie on this line. Draw the line on a graph and check that your list is correct.

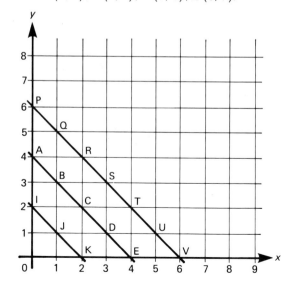

C Write down the co-ordinates of the corners of the shapes in the figure. See if you can find a 'clue' in the co-ordinates which would tell you about the shape, for example whether opposite sides are equal.

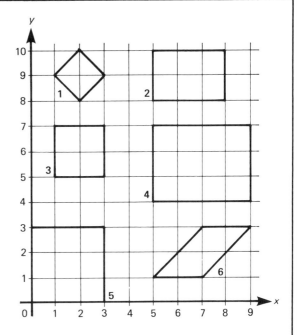

Extension of the graph

A graph can be extended by using **negative numbers**. Extend the x axis towards the left and the y axis downwards and mark the numbers with a negative sign.

Example:

In the diagram below the co-ordinates of A are $(-1, 3)$, co-ordinates of C are $(-3, -2)$

Note: The x co-ordinate is given first.

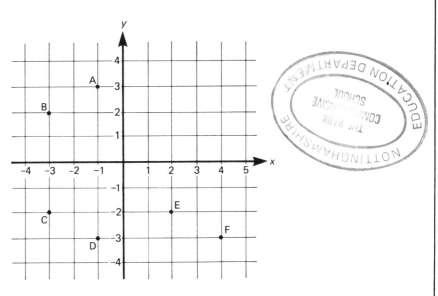

89

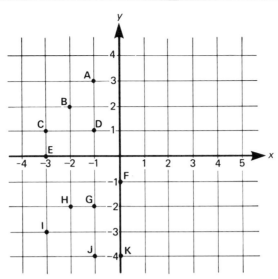

Exercise M81

A 1 Write down the co-ordinates of the points A, B, C, D, E, F in the above figure.

2 What words correspond to these sets of co-ordinates?
$(-2, 2); (-1, 3); (-1, 1)$ $(-2, 2); (-1, 3); (-3, 1); (0, -4)$
$(-2, -2); (-3, -3); (-1, 1); (-3, 0)$

B 1 The points A, D, G, J all lie on the same line, which is parallel to the y axis. How does this show up in the co-ordinates of the points?

2 Where would you expect to find points whose x co-ordinates and y co-ordinates are equal, e.g., $(-3, -3); (-5, -5)$?

3 Plot ten different points where the x co-ordinate and the y co-ordinate add up to zero, e.g., $(3, -3); (-4, 4)$. Which lines do all these points lie on?

C What shape do you make if you join up all these points?

1 $(2, 2); (2, -2); (-2, 2); (-2, -2)$

2 $(2, 3); (2, -3); (-2, 3); (-2, -3)$

3 $(2, 0); (0, 2); (-2, 0); (0, -2)$

4 $(1, 0); (0, 2); (-1, 0); (0, -2)$

5 $(2, 2); (-2, 2); (-3, -2); (3, -2)$

D 1 This figure has the y axis as an axis of symmetry. Find the co-ordinates of the points:

A and B
C and D
E and F
G and H

What do you notice?
Such points are **reflections** in the y axis.

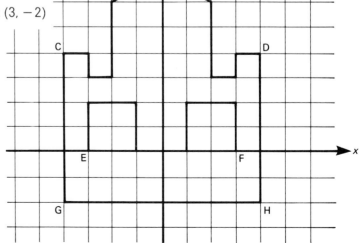

2 Draw a figure for which the x axis is an axis of symmetry. Check the co-ordinates of the pairs of points which are reflections in the x axis.

Graph of a function

If we start with the numbers $(1, 2, 3, \ldots, 10)$ and then add 3 to each number we get a new set $(4, 5, 6, \ldots, 13)$.
This is an example of a **linear function**.

We can write it as $x \rightarrow x + 3$ or $y = x + 3$

Both these ways of writing functions are important.

If we now form pairs by taking a number and its image under the mapping we get a set of **ordered** pairs. These, used as co-ordinates, will give the graph of the function, $x \rightarrow x + 3$.

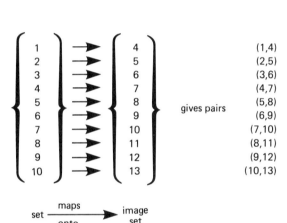

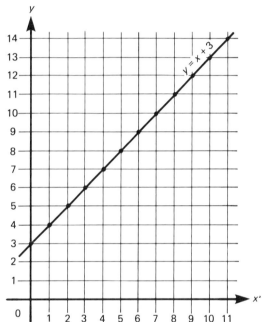

Exercise M82

A Write down the image set of $(1, 2, 3, 4, 5, 6, 7, 8, 9, 10)$ under these mappings.

   1 $x \rightarrow x + 2$ **2** $x \rightarrow x + 5$ **3** $x \rightarrow x + 10$

   4 $x \rightarrow x - 1$ **5** $x \rightarrow x - 5$ **6** $x \rightarrow x - 10$

B Write down all the ordered pairs which arise from each mapping in part **A**.

C Using the ordered pairs of question **B**, draw these graphs.

   1 $y = x + 2$ **2** $y = x + 5$ **3** $y = x + 10$

   4 $y = x - 1$ **5** $y = x - 5$ **6** $y = x - 10$

What do you notice about all these graphs?

Unit M22   Percentages

A special family of fractions

Fractions such as 2/100, 14/100, 50/100 are called **percentage fractions**. There is a special sign that is used called the percentage sign, % ('per cent' comes from the Latin word for 100, *centum*).

Example:

2% ↔ 2/100 ↔ 2 per cent or two parts out of every hundred

Exercise M83

A   Write these in percentage form and in words.

1	3/100	**2**	5/100	**3**	10/100	**4**	25/100
5	50/100	**6**	66/100	**7**	12.5/100	**8**	99/100

B   Write these in fraction form and in words.

1	2%	**2**	10%	**3**	22%	**4**	30%
5	50%	**6**	75%	**7**	90%	**8**	100%

C   Explain what these sentences mean.

1   John is asleep 50% of the time.

2   This sweater is 100% wool.

3   I am 99% sure that Granny will come this weekend.

4   The loaf is 100% wholewheat.

5   Margaret got 70% right in the test.

Decimal form (value)

Every percentage has a decimal form obtained by working out the division by 100.

Examples:

(a) 50% ↔ 50/100 ↔ 0·5   (b) 37·5% ↔ 37·5/100 ↔ 0·375

Exercise M84

A   Write these percentages in decimal form.

1 20%   **2** 25%   **3** 40%   **4** 42%   **5** 55%

6 99%   **7** 75%   **8** 36%   **9** 2·5%   **10** 12·8%

B   Write these decimals as percentages.

1 0·45   **2** 0·77   **3** 0·85   **4** 0·96

5 1·25   **6** 0·15   **7** 0·015   **8** 0·375

C   Write these common fractions in percentage form. You will have to put them in decimal form first.

Example: 3/4, three-quarters ↔ 0·75 ↔ 75%

1 1/4   **2** 1/2   **3** 3/8   **4** 5/8   **5** $1\frac{1}{2}$

6 2/3   **7** 7/8   **8** 9/10   **9** 5/12   **10** 4/5

Use of percentages for comparison

Percentages are often used to compare two sets.

Example: There were 14 boys and 16 girls in class 1G. 9 of the boys had had measles and 10 of the girls had had measles.

Boys with measles 9/14 → 0·64 → 64%; Girls with measles 10/16 → 0·625 → 62·5%

Conclusion: A higher percentage of boys have had measles than girls.

Exercise M85

1   Two rings are made of gold and silver mixed. The first ring weighs 60 g and contains 35 g of gold. The second ring has 27 g of gold and weighs 52 g. Which ring has the higher percentage of gold?

2   A bicycle shop sold two types of bikes, Whizzer and Cruiser. In one month 40 Whizzers and 28 Cruisers were sold. 5 Whizzers and 3 Cruisers were brought back to the shop because something was wrong. Which type had the higher percentage of faulty bikes?

3   Mrs King had 12 children. She bought 24 pairs of woollen socks and 30 pairs of nylon/wool mixture socks. After one month 3 pairs of woollen socks and 4 pairs of nylon/wool socks had holes. Comment.

4   Billy Brown got 42 out of 60 in a French test and 55 out of 80 in a Science test. At which subject was Billy better?

5   75 girls and 90 boys were asked if they liked dogs better than cats. 56 girls and 67 boys said yes. What percentage of boys and of girls prefer dogs?

Finding actual numbers from percentages

Example:

In a class of 30 children, 80% had been vaccinated. How many children had not been vaccinated?

80% of 30 → 0·80 × 30 → 24 vaccinated

          30 − 24   → 6 not vaccinated

NOTE: '80% of' becomes '0·80 ×'

Exercise M86

A **1** In a class of 32, 87·5% of the pupils were 12 years or over. How many children were under 12 years?

2 In a club of 75 children, 40% were girls. How many boys?

3 A gardener has 40% of his lettuces in the greenhouse. He plants 150 lettuces. How many are out in the open?

4 John spends 40% of his TV viewing time in a week watching sport. If he watches about 30 hours a week altogether, how many hours of sport does he watch? How many hours does he spend watching other things?

5 Liz went on a journey by bike. The whole journey was 150 km. She cycled 22% of the journey on the first day. How much further did she have to go?

6 All children study for 24 hours a week in school. 17% of this time is spent on Maths. How many hours are spent on other subjects?

B Example:

20 children in a class could swim. This was 62·5%. How many children are there in the class?

Suppose there are n children in the class.

62·5% of $n \rightarrow n \times 0.625 = 20$

We need a number which when multiplied by 0·625 gives 20.

The number must be 20/0·625 (because 20/0·625 × 0·625 = 20)

There are 32 children in the class

Check: 20/32 = 0·625 = 62·5%

1 24 children in a class eat school dinner. This is 80% of the children. How many children are there in the class?

2 36 children were absent from school on Tuesday. This was 12%. How many children are there in the school?

3 10% of a crate of oranges had split skins. The other 108 oranges were OK. How many oranges were there altogether?

4 In a battle, 25% of the soldiers were killed or wounded. 3300 were unhurt. How many took part in the battle?

5 78% of the children in a school had fillings in their teeth. What percentage did not have fillings? If, in fact, 198 children had no fillings, how many children were there in the school?

6 A moon rocket used 28% of its fuel to leave the earth. If it had 4200 gallons of fuel left, how much fuel did it start with?

C Work out these.

1	20% of £10	**2**	66% of £48	**3**	15% of 2 m
4	36% of 75 litres	**5**	17% of £1·40	**6**	50% of £66
7	23% of £2·80	**8**	37% of 5 km	**9**	72% of 25 kg
10	30% of £45	**11**	120% of 88 hours	**12**	1·5% of 980 miles

Unit M23 Algebra

Reversing a sequence

The calculator 'does things' to numbers when you press the operation keys. You can 'undo' the operations, if you think carefully, and work back to the number you started with.

- − undoes +   ÷ undoes ×
- + undoes −   × undoes ÷

Examples:

(a)

	Forward	Reverse
	$7 + 5 = 12$	$12 - 5 = 7$
	7 + 5 =	1 2 − 5 =
Display	7 7 5 12	12 12 5 7

(b)

Forward
$16 \div 7 = 2.285\ 714\ 2$

1 6 ÷ 7 =

Display   16 16 7 ↑
                    2.285 714 2

Reverse
$2.285\ 714\ 2 \times 7$

☐ × 7 =

↑ 7 15.999 999

Note: The calculator gives back *15.999 999* instead of *16*. This is just the calculator's second way of saying *16* on the display.

Exercise M87

A First work out the values. Then write down the calculator sequence which will undo these addition and subtraction sums and give back the number you started with (marked with a star*).

1 *8 + 3 =   **2** *17 − 5 =   **3** *42 + 17 =

4 *36 − 14 =   **5** *75 + 11·2 =   **6** *4·7 − 0·6 =

B Repeat question **A** for these multiplications and divisions.

1 *8 × 3 =   **2** *4 × 5 =   **3** *11 × 35 =   **4** *61 × 99 =

5 *9 ÷ 3 =   **6** *14 ÷ 2 =   **7** *20 ÷ 8 =   **8** *39 ÷ 15 =

9 *3·6 ÷ ·5 =   **10** *2·8 × 1·2 =   **11** *55 ÷ ·3 =   **12** *408 × 0·35 =

C Working backwards can answer questions.

Example:

I put a number in the calculator, pressed ⊞, ①⓪ and ⊟. The display showed *92*. What number was put in?

Forwards

$\boxed{n}\ \boxed{+}\ \boxed{1}\ \boxed{0}\ \boxed{=}$ $\boxed{-}\ \boxed{1}\ \boxed{0}\ \boxed{=}$

  92   *92   10   82*

                   ↑ *This must be n*

Find *n* for each of these.

		Display			Display			Display
1	$n + 2 =$	*12*	**2**	$n + 12 =$	*20*	**3**	$n - 32 =$	*56·4*
4	$n - 1·1 =$	*3·9*	**5**	$n \times 3 =$	*30*	**6**	$n \times 1·4 =$	*9·8*
7	$n \div 10 =$	*5*	**8**	$n \div 4·2 =$	*23*			

Equations

Example:

$x + 3 = 5$

This simple number sentence is true if *x* is 2.

Such sentences are called **equations**, and finding a value for *x* which makes them true is called **solving** the equation.

Exercise M88

A Find values for *x* which make these equations true.

1 $x + 3 = 6$		**2** $x + 4 = 9$		**3** $x - 5 = 4$
4 $x - 2 = 6$		**5** $x + 10 = 20$		**6** $x + 10 = 50$
7 $x - 10 = 40$		**8** $x - 20 = 70$		**9** $x + 200 = 300$
10 $x + 400 = 800$		**11** $x - 100 = 700$		**12** $x - 300 = 500$

B Equations can also have × and ÷ in them. Find the values for *x* which make these true.

1 $2 \times x = 8$	**2** $2 \times x = 10$	**3** $3 \times x = 12$	**4** $5 \times x = 20$
5 $x \div 2 = 4$	**6** $x \div 3 = 3$	**7** $x \div 5 = 3$	**8** $x \div 10 = 2$
9 $x \times 5 = 5$	**10** $x \times 3 = 15$	**11** $x \times 4 = 24$	**12** $x \times 10 = 40$
13 $16 \div x = 4$	**14** $20 \div x = 5$	**15** $25 \div x = 5$	**16** $100 \div x = 10$

C If the numbers are bigger, the calculator should be used.

Example:

$x + 2·42 = 3·61$

$\boxed{3}\ \boxed{.}\ \boxed{6}\ \boxed{1}\ \boxed{-}\ \boxed{2}\ \boxed{.}\ \boxed{4}\ \boxed{2}\ \boxed{=}\ 1·19$

Check: $1·19 + 2·42 = 3·61$

Putting 1·19 for *x* makes the equation true.

Find values of x which make these true. (Use machine.)

1 $x + 3.4 = 4.5$ **2** $x + 2.71 = 5.24$ **3** $x + 4.09 = 6.22$

4 $x + 3.6 = 10$ **5** $x - 5.1 = 11$ **6** $x - 0.23 = 1.4$

7 $x - 1.15 = 2.304$ **8** $x - 4.04 = 14.04$ **9** $x \times 3.7 = 18.5$

10 $x \times 1.94 = 5.82$ **11** $x \times 0.33 = 1.65$ **12** $x \times 1.32 = 15.84$

13 $x \div 4.2 = 5$ **14** $x \div 6 = 3.7$ **15** $x \div 3.5 = 1.4$

16 $x \div 1.26 = 3.11$

Forming an equation

Many problems can be put in equation form and then solved.

Examples:

(a) I think of a number and double it. The answer is 16.
What was the number?

Equation: $x \times 2 = 16$.

(b) I went shopping with £10 and came home with £4.50.
How much did I spend?

Equation: $x + 4.50 = 10$

Forming an equation is more than half-way to solving a problem.

Exercise M89

A   Form equations from these sentences.

1   I think of a number and add 3 to it. The result is 10. What was the number?

2   I have £6. My mother has promised me some money. When I have it I will have £11. How much has she promised?

3   The temperature at midday is 24°C. This morning it was 19°C. How much has it risen?

4   John lost 3 teeth in a fight. He had 24 when the fight started. How many has he now?

5   Two similar chocolate Easter eggs cost 140p. What does one cost?

6   Three rabbits need 600 g of food a day. What does one rabbit need?

7   Three girls earned £1.50 each for one evening babysitting. How much did they earn together?

8   Linda swam for 120 lengths in the pool. If she swims 40 lengths an hour, how long did her swim take?

B   Write 'stories' for these equations.

1 $x + 2 = 7$ **2** $3 + x = 7$ **3** $x - 5 = 20$ **4** $x - 10 = 22$

5 $3 \times x = 18$ **6** $5 \times x = 50$ **7** $x \times 4 = 16$ **8** $x \times 3 = 15$

9 $x \div 10 = 2$ **10** $x \div 5 = 3$ **11** $100 \div x = 2$ **12** $50 \div x = 5$

Special forms of x

We always write $2 \times x$ as $2x$, $3 \times x$ as $3x$. So never get mixed up between $2x$ and $2 + x$.

We write $x \times x$ as x^2, $x \times x \times x$ as x^3, $x \times x \times x \times x$ as x^4.

Example:

If x is 10, $2 + x = 12$
$$2x = 20$$
x^2 is $10 \times 10 = 100$
$$2x + 4 = 24$$

Exercise M89A

A Which of these are true when $x = 2$?

1 $x + 3 = 5$	**2** $x + 7 = 8$	**3** $x + 12 = 14$	**4** $x + 1 = 4$
5 $2x = 4$	**6** $3x = 9$	**7** $4x = 8$	**8** $5x = 12$
9 $x^2 = 4$	**10** $x^3 = 8$	**11** $x^4 = 12$	**12** $2x + 3 = 8$
13 $3x + 5 = 11$	**14** $2x - 4 = 2$	**15** $3x - 1 = 4$	**16** $x^3 - 2 = 0$

B Find which of each pair is larger.

1 x^2 or $2x$ when $x = 3$

2 $x + 2$ or $2x$ when $x = 3$

3 $2x + 4$ or $3x$ when $x = 3$

4 $3x$ or x^3 when $x = 3$

5 $x + x$ or $2x$ when $x = 5$

6 $3x - 2$ or x^2 when $x = 4$

7 $4x + 3$ or $x^2 + 2$ when $x = 5$

8 $6x - 3$ or x^2 when $x = 5$

9 x^3 or $6x$ when $x = 4$

10 x^3 or $2x^2$ when $x = 10$

11 $x^2 - 10$ or $x + 2$ when $x = 6$

12 $x^2 + 3$ or $4x + 3$ when $x = 2$

C Find which of these are true when $x = 3.45$.

1 $x + 3 = 6.45$	**2** $x + 5 = 8.45$	**3** $x - 4 = 2.45$
4 $x + 2.6 = 8.05$	**5** $x - 3.25 = 0.2$	**6** $2x = 6.9$
7 $3x + 1 = 11.35$	**8** $x^2 = 11.9025$	**9** $x^2 + 3 = 14.9$
10 $x^3 = 10.35$	**11** $x^2 + x = 15.3525$	**12** $2x + x = 10.35$
13 $5x - 4 = 13.65$	**14** $x^2 + 2x = 10.35$	**15** $x^2 + x^3 = 10.005$
16 $4x - x^2 = 1.8975$		

Unit M24   Factors and primes

Factors, multiples, primes

Some numbers can be divided by others without leaving any remainder.

When this happens the dividing number is called a **factor** of the divided number.

Examples:

(a) $12/6 = 2$ 6 is a factor of 12 (and so is 2)
(b) $20/3 = 6.666\,6$ so 3 is not a factor of 20
(c) $20/5 = 4$ 5 is a factor of 20 (and so is 4)
(d) $684/36 = 19$ 36 is a factor of 684 (and so is 19)

General rule

If $n/a \rightarrow b$, where a and b are both whole numbers, then a and b are factors of n.

Exercise M90

A 1   Which of 2, 3, 4 and 5 are factors of 28? What other factors can you find of 28?

2   Find all the factors of 48. (There are eight of them!)

3   Find all the factors of 56, 100 and 150.

4   Find a number that has 2, 3, 4, 5 and 6 for factors.

B   In which of the following is the dividing number a factor?

1 30/15	**2** 36/12	**3** 55/10	**4** 72/32	**5** 100/4
6 115/7	**7** 240/16	**8** 529/23	**9** 266/17	**10** 1001/7

C   Find two factors of each of these numbers.

1 49	**2** 102	**3** 111	**4** 132	**5** 75
6 100	**7** 144	**8** 121	**9** 177	**10** 290

Spotting factors

It is very easy to spot some factors of numbers. Look carefully at these rules.

Example	Test	Factor
140	Does the number end in 0?	10 is a factor
178	Is the number even?	2 is a factor
195	Does the number end in 5 or 0?	5 is a factor
324	Are the last two numbers part of the 4 × table?	4 is a factor
411	Do the 'figures' of the number add to 3, 6 or 9?	3 is a factor
414	Do the 'figures' of the number add up to 9?	9 is a factor
222	Is the number even and is 3 a factor?	6 is a factor

Exercise M91

A Use the rules to 'spot' one factor for each of these numbers.

1 4850	**2** 485	**3** 2666	**4** 5174
5 81	**6** 111	**7** 213	**8** 2001

B Use the rules to spot as many factors as you can for each of these numbers. Check on the calculator.

1 560	**2** 288	**3** 729	**4** 1500	**5** 1000
6 1728	**7** 360	**8** 4932	**9** 5004	**10** 6543

When two numbers are multiplied, **multiples** are formed.

Examples:

(a) 6, 9, 12, 15, 30, 300 are some of the multiples of 3.
(b) 15, 25, 40, 75, 125 are some of the multiples of 5.

Multiples and factors are related.

Examples:

(a) 3 is a factor of 12; 12 is a multiple of 3.
(b) 5 is a factor of 100; 100 is a multiple of 5.
This is like mother/child.

General rule: If x is a **factor** of n, then n is a **multiple** of x.

Exercise M92

A Put the correct word 'factor' or 'multiple' into these sentences.

1 4 is a . . . of 16	**2** 20 is a . . . of 5	**3** 20 is a . . . of 100
4 15 is a . . . of 225	**5** 75 is a . . . of 25	**6** 100 is a . . . of 1000
7 150 is a . . . of 50	**8** 250 is a . . . of 1000	

B **1** Which of these numbers are not multiples of 3?
21, 34, 69, 84, 100, 106, 144, 291

    2 Which of these numbers are not multiples of 9?
81, 167, 233, 450, 656. 711, 1010

    3 Which of these numbers are not multiples of 4?
42, 82, 96, 132, 256, 412, 720

Prime numbers

If a number has no factors it is called a **prime** number.

Example:

13 is a prime number.

$13/2 \rightarrow 6.5$	$13/6 \rightarrow 2.1666\ldots$	$13/10 \rightarrow 1.3$
$13/3 \rightarrow 4.3333\ldots$	$13/7 \rightarrow 1.8571\ldots$	$13/11 \rightarrow 1.1818$
$13/4 \rightarrow 3.25$	$13/8 \rightarrow 1.625$	$13/12 \rightarrow 1.0833$
$13/5 \rightarrow 2.6$	$13/9 \rightarrow 1.4444$	

No number divides 13 exactly leaving no remainder. (*Except 13 itself.*)

Exercise M93

A **1** Show that these numbers are prime numbers.
11, 17, 23.

2 Pick out the prime numbers from these.
2, 7, 9, 14, 21, 32, 33, 45, 51, 53, 70.

3 Explain why a number ending in 5 cannot be a prime.

B Make a list of the prime numbers below 20. Do any of them divide 373? Why is this a test to see whether 373 is a prime?
(*Hint:* 20 × 20 = 400. If one factor is bigger than 20, the other must be less than 20.)

C Find out whether these numbers are prime numbers. 91, 133, 189, 203.

The prime factors of a number

A number like 42 can be written as 7 × 6.

The 7 is a prime but the 6 can be split into prime factors.

$42 \rightarrow 7 \times 6 \rightarrow 7 \times 3 \times 2$. This is the prime factor form of 42.

Exercise M94

A Put these numbers into prime factor form.

1	14	**2**	30	**3**	48	**4**	63
5	77	**6**	90	**7**	128	**8**	180

B Follow this programme carefully to find prime factors of any number.

1 Divide by 2 again and again until the result is no longer a multiple of 2.

2 Divide by 3 until the result is no longer a multiple of 3.

3 Divide by 5 until the result is no longer a multiple of 5.

and so on, going to the next prime number each time, 7, 11 etc.

When the result is 1, collect up all the numbers you have divided by. These are the prime factors.

Use the programme to find the prime factors of

1 100 **2** 240 **3** 380 **4** 526 **5** 999

Unit M25 Problem solving II

Searching for a pattern

Where a problem has to be solved, first we collect information and
then we 'search' it for clues. These clues may be in the form of
patterns. When looking for patterns we look for:

1 Repeats

2 Connections

3 Steady changes

Example:

What is the next of these numbers: 1, 2, 4, 7, 11, ...?

When we look carefully we see
that the next number must
be $11 + 5 = 16$

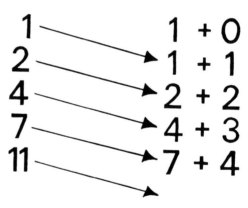

Another way is to notice that each number grows by one more each time:

$$\begin{array}{ccccc} & +1 & +2 & +3 & +4 \\ 1 & \!\!\frown\!\! 2 & \!\!\frown\!\! 4 & \!\!\frown\!\! 7 & \!\!\frown\!\! 11 \ldots \end{array}$$

Exercise M95

A Find the next number in each of these **sequences***.

1	1, 2, 3, 4, 5, 6, ?	**2**	1, 3, 5, 7, 9, 11, ?	**3**	2, 4, 6, 8, 10, 12, ?
4	5, 10, 15, 20, 25, 30, ?	**5**	1, 1, 2, 4, 7, 11, ?	**6**	3, 4, 7, 12, 19, 28, ?
7	1, 1, 2, 3, 5, 8, ?	**8**	1, 4, 9, 16, 25, ?	**9**	10, 20, 30, 40, 50, ?
10	31, 28, 25, 22, 19, ?	**11**	2, 6, 12, 20, 30, ?	**12**	64, 32, 16, 8, 4, ?

*A sequence is a set of numbers arranged in order.

B   Many patterns can be seen when you divide numbers.

Example:

1/3 → 0·333 333 . . . (recurring decimal)

Write down the patterns you see in the values of these fractions.

1 1/6	**2** 2/6	**3** 4/9	**4** 7/9	**5** 5/3	**6** 20/9
7 3/7	**8** 1/7	**9** 5/7	**10** 1/11	**11** 3/11	**12** 5/11

C   In a sequence, each number is connected to its position in the sequence.

Example:
$$\left\{ \begin{matrix} 1 & 2 & 3 & 4 & 5 & 6 & 7 & 8 & 9 & \leftarrow\text{place in sequence} \\ 3 & 5 & 7 & 9 & 11 & 13 & 15 & 17 & 19 & \leftarrow\text{numbers in sequence} \end{matrix} \right\}$$

The number can be found by **doubling** the **place** and adding 1.

$(2 \times 1) + 1 \rightarrow 3$ $(2 \times 2) + 1 \rightarrow 5$ $(2 \times 3) + 1 \rightarrow 7$

and so on.

This will tell you that the 100th number is $(2 \times 100) + 1 \rightarrow 201$ and so on.

Find the connection between the numbers of these sequences and their places. Then find the 100th number of the sequence.

1 2, 4, 6, 8, 10 . . .	**2** 7, 9, 11, 13, 15 . . .	**3** 4, 6, 8, 10, 12 . . .
4 4, 7, 10, 13, 16 . . .	**5** 5, 10, 15, 20, 25 . . .	**6** 6, 11, 16, 21, 26
7 1, 3, 5, 7, 9 . . .	**8** 3, 6, 9, 12, 15 . . .	**9** 5, 8, 11, 14, 17 . . .
10 4, 9, 14, 19, 24 . . .	**11** 12, 22, 32, 42, 52 . . .	**12** 9, 19, 29, 39, 49 . . .

Patterns in shapes

When searching shapes for patterns:

1   Look for things which stay the same.

2   Look for the way the shapes connect with each other.

3   Look for rules which would help you draw new shapes.

Example:

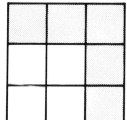

These three shapes are:

1   all squares

2   all made up from square units

3   each new shape is made from the one before by adding squares round two sides.

Exercise M96

A Look carefully at these patterns. Write down all the facts which seem important.

1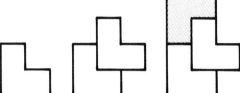

2

3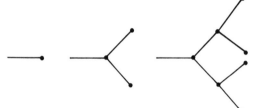

4

5

6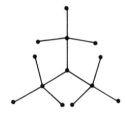

B Sort out the different shapes you can find in these diagrams. Measure them carefully.

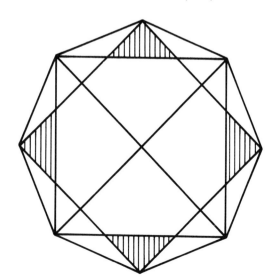

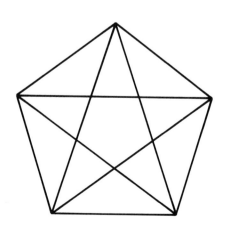

C The most important patterns we learn are those of the letters of the alphabet.

Look carefully at the capital and small letters* and answer the questions.

ABCDEFGHIJKLMNOPQRSTUVWXYZ
abcdefghijklmnopqrstuvwxyz

1 Which capital letters are made from straight lines only?

2 Which lower case letters are made from straight lines only?

3 Which capital letters are made from curved lines only?

4 Which lower case letters are made from curved lines only?

5 Which capital letters have enclosed spaces?

e.g.: **A**————enclosed space

6 Which lower case letters have enclosed spaces?

Is it true that:

7 All capitals made of straight lines only have corresponding lower case letters made of straight lines only?

8 All lower case letters with enclosed spaces correspond to capitals with enclosed spaces?

*Small letters are called lower case.

Everyday patterns

Our ordinary lives follow many patterns. Here are some examples:

1 breakfast, lunch, tea, supper, breakfast, lunch, tea, . . .
2 Sunday, Monday, Tuesday, Wednesday, . . .

Exercise M97
A Which patterns do you connect with these?

1 the time of year	2 the game of football	3 swimming
4 life on a farm	5 travelling by train	6 school

B Answer these questions about patterns. (You may have to use the library.)

1 Every four years, we have an extra day, 29 February. These years are called leap years. Why does this happen?

2 Human beings follow the life pattern: baby, child, adult, old person. What is the life pattern of an insect?

3 Every time you make a pot of tea, you probably follow a certain pattern. Write it down. Ask a friend if you have left anything out.

4 Each month the moon follows a certain pattern. Why does this happen?

Unit M26 Brackets and the calculator

Brackets and calculator

You are asked to work out $2 + 3 \times 5$. The answer depends on whether you multiply or add first.

$2 + 3 \times 5$

$\quad 5 \quad \times 5 = 25 \quad$ (Your calculator would get this result.)

$2 + 3 \times 5$

$\quad 2 + \quad 15 \quad = 17 \quad$ (Ordinary rules of arithmetic would expect this.)

We can avoid this choice of answers by using **brackets**. Everything inside brackets is worked out first.

$2 + (3 \times 5) \rightarrow 2 + 15 \rightarrow 17 \qquad$ This can only be 17
$(2 + 3) \times 5 \rightarrow 5 \times 5 \rightarrow 25 \qquad$ This can only be 25

Exercise M98

A By using different orders of working out, find several possible values for these.

1 $2 + 4 \times 3$	**2** $3 \times 5 - 2$	**3** $6 - 4 \times 2$	**4** $4 \times 6 + 3$
5 $5 + 4 \times 3$	**6** $7 - 2 \times 5$	**7** $4 \div 2 \times 2$	**8** $5 \times 3 \div 5$
9 $10 \div 2 \times 4$	**10** $6 \div 3 \div 2$	**11** $12 \div 4 + 3$	**12** $4 + 3 \div 2$

B Work out these. Remember to work out the brackets first.

1 $(3 + 7) \times 2$	**2** $5 \times (4 - 3)$	**3** $6 + (6 \times 6)$
4 $10 + (3 \times 5)$	**5** $8 + (4 - 2)$	**6** $(12 - 3) + 4$
7 $(8 - 4) - 2$	**8** $10 - (7 - 3)$	**9** $(12 - 5) \times 2$
10 $15 - (5 \times 3)$	**11** $6 \div (3 \times 3)$	**12** $(10 \div 2) + 4$
13 $15 - (5 \div 5)$	**14** $(18 - 4) \div 7$	**15** $(20 \div 4) \times 2$
16 $30 \div (3 \times 5)$		

C Add brackets to make these correct.

Example:

$7 + 9 \times 3 = 34 ; 7 + (9 \times 3) = 34$

1 $4 + 3 \times 7 = 25$	**2** $5 + 5 \times 5 = 50$	**3** $4 + 3 - 1 = 6$
4 $12 - 6 - 3 = 9$	**5** $7 + 3 - 4 = 6$	**6** $3 \times 4 \times 2 = 24$

7 $8 \div 4 \times 2 = 1$ **8** $12 \div 4 + 2 = 5$ **9** $8 \div 4 + 2 = 4$

10 $6 \times 5 \div 10 = 3$ **11** $16 \div 8 - 2 = 0$ **12** $20 - 10 \div 5 = 18$

Calculator language

When you are 'talking to' your calculator, remember that it cannot think. It simply follows your instructions in the order you give them.*

Example:

$\boxed{C}$ $\boxed{4}$ $\boxed{+}$ $\boxed{3}$ $\boxed{\times}$ $\boxed{7}$ $\boxed{=}$ $\rightarrow 49$
0   4   4   3   7   7   49

If you want to work out $4 + (3 \times 7)$ you have to present it to the calculator as $3 \times 7 + 4$:

$\boxed{C}$ $\boxed{3}$ $\boxed{\times}$ $\boxed{7}$ $\boxed{+}$ $\boxed{4}$ $\boxed{=}$ $\rightarrow 25$
0   3   3   7   21   4   25

Exercise M99

A Rewrite these calculations (where necessary) so that the calculator gives the same result as working by the rules of arithmetic.

   1 $2 + 5 \times 3$ **2** $14 - 5 - 2$ **3** $7 + 4 \times 2$ **4** $8 \times 4 + 3$

   5 $8 \div 4 \times 2$ **6** $2 + 3 \div 5$ **7** $5 + 5 \times 5$ **8** $6 + 6 \div 6$

B Use the calculator to get the results of these calculations. Remember in some cases you will have to change the order. Estimate each one roughly as a check.

   1 $3 + (5 \times 6)$ **2** $(14 + 3) \times 7$ **3** $(7 \times 9) \times 6$

   4 $2 + (6 \times 3)$ **5** $10 \times (10 + 10)$ **6** $10 \times (3 + 4)$

   7 $(1 \cdot 6 + 3 \cdot 4) \times 10$ **8** $2 \cdot 1 + (1 \cdot 5 \times 3)$ **9** $4 \cdot 4 \times (4 \cdot 4 + 4 \cdot 4)$

   10 $3 \cdot 6 \div (4 + 9)$ **11** $14 + (6 \div 4 \cdot 2)$ **12** $20 \div (3 \div 2)$

C Write these sentences in numbers and work them out on the calculator.

   1 I added six to nine and then multiplied the result by seven.

   2 I multiplied six by ten and added two.

   3 I added five to ten multiplied by six.

   4 I added three point seven to twenty-two multiplied by six.

   5 I divided three into seven plus eight.

   6 I divided four plus twenty by six.

   7 I divided fifty-four by nine and then subtracted six.

   8 I took ten from thirty-two times four point five.

   9 I took one point eight from seventeen divided by six.

   10 I divided forty-four by six and then divided by three.

* Some calculators are programmed to use brackets and to follow arithmetical language.

Algebra

We can talk about machine language by using letters for numbers.

Example:

We know that $3 + 5 = 5 + 3$, and $2 + 7 = 7 + 2$ and so on.

In general, $a + b = b + a$ where a, b are numbers.

We use ab as short for $a \times b$ (the product of multiplying two numbers a and b).

Exercise M100

A Choose numbers for a, b and c to check the truth of these. (Use the calculator.)

Example:

Check $a \div b = b \div a$

Let $\left.\begin{matrix} a = 1.75 \\ b = 3.82 \end{matrix}\right\}$ (chosen at random) $\quad \begin{matrix} a \div b = 0.458 \\ b \div a = 2.183 \end{matrix}$

Therefore $a \div b = b \div a$ is **not true**

1 $a + b = b + a$		**2** $a - b = b - a$	
3 $a \times b = b \times a$		**4** $a \div b = b \div a$	
5 $a + (b + c) = (a + b) + c$		**6** $a + (b - c) = (a + b) - c$	
7 $a - (b - c) = (a - b) - c$		**8** $a + (b \times c) = (a + b) \times c$	
9 $a \times (b \times c) = (a \times b) \times c$		**10** $a \times (b - c) = (a \times b) - c$	
11 $(a \div b) \times c = a \div (b \times c)$		**12** $(a \div b) \div c = a \div (b \div c)$	

B Remembering that ab is the same as $a \times b$ (because in algebra the multiplication sign is left out to avoid mixing it up with x), check whether these statements are true by replacing a, b and c by numbers.

1 $ab = ba$

2 $(ab)c = a(bc)$

3 $a(b + c) = ab + ac$

4 $a + (bc) = (a + b)(a + c)$

5 $a - (bc) = (a - b)c$

6 $a(b - c) = ab - ac$

7 $(a + b)c = ac + bc$

8 $(a - b)c = ac - bc$

9 $(a + b) \div c = (a \div c) + (b \div c)$

C We write $a \times a$ as a^2 for short,* and $(a + b) \times (a + b)$ as $(a + b)^2$.

Examples:

If $a = 5$ then $a^2 = 25$, If $a = 2.3$ then $a^2 = 5.29$

Use numbers and the calculator to check the truth of these.

1 $a(a + 1) = a^2 + a$

2 $a(a - 1) = a^2 - a$

3 $a + a = 2 \times a$

4 $2 \times a \times a = a^2 \times 2$

5 $a \times (a + 2) = a^2 + 2$

6 $a(a + b) = a^2 + ab$

* Invented by a great mathematician named Liebniz.

108

7 $a(a - b) = a^2 - ab$

8 $a^2 + b^2 = (a + b)^2$

9 $(a + b)^2 = a^2 + b^2 + 2ab$

10 $(a - b)^2 = a^2 - b^2$

11 $(a + b)(a - b) = a^2 - b^2$

12 $(a - b)^2 = a^2 + b^2 - 2ab$

Note: For these questions you should lay out your work carefully.

Example:

To check: $a(a + b) = a^2 + ab$

Let: $a = 2 \cdot 3$ $b = 3 \cdot 7$

Calculator steps:

$$a + b = 6 \cdot 0$$
$$a(a + b) = 2 \cdot 3 \times 6 \cdot 0$$
$$= 13 \cdot 8$$

$$a^2 = 2 \cdot 3 \times 2 \cdot 3 = 5 \cdot 29$$
$$ab = 2 \cdot 3 \times 3 \cdot 7 = 8 \cdot 51$$
$$a^2 + ab = 5 \cdot 29 + 8 \cdot 51 = 13 \cdot 8$$

Diagrams for brackets

We can use diagrams on squared paper to show some of the bracket rules. We show single numbers, $+$ and $-$ as lengths, and products as areas.

Examples:

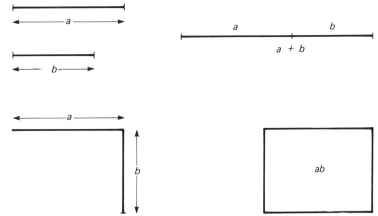

This follows from the rule for finding areas of rectangles.

Exercise M101

A Look carefully at each of the diagrams and make sure you can see how it shows the algebra.

1

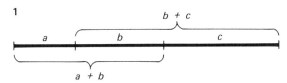

This shows $(a + b) + c = a + (b + c)$

2

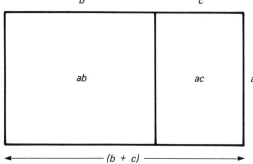

This shows $a(b + c) = ab + ac$

B Match up these diagrams with the correct algebra.

1

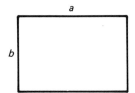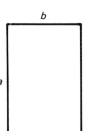

2

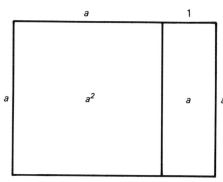

3

4

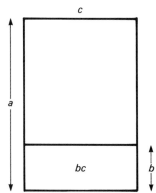

Algebra: $a + b = b + a$
$ab = ba$
$a(a + 1) = a^2 + a$
$(a - b)c = ac - bc$

C Using squared paper, draw diagrams to show each of these.

1 $a(a + 3) = a^2 + 3a$ **2** $(a + b) + c = (a + c) + b$

3 $2(a + b) = 2a + 2b$ **4** $3a - 3b = 3(a - b)$

5 $(a + b)c = ac + bc$ **6** $a + 2a = 3a$

7 $2a - 2 = 2(a - 1)$ **8** $(a + 1)^2 = a^2 + 2a + 1$

9 $(a + b)^2 = a^2 + 2ab + b^2$

Unit M27   Scale

Enlargement and scale

When a photograph is enlarged, all the lengths are enlarged on the same **scale**.

The fraction formed from two corresponding measurements is called the **scale factor**.

d_2/d_1 is the scale factor of the enlargement in the figure.

All other lines will be enlarged by the same scale factor.

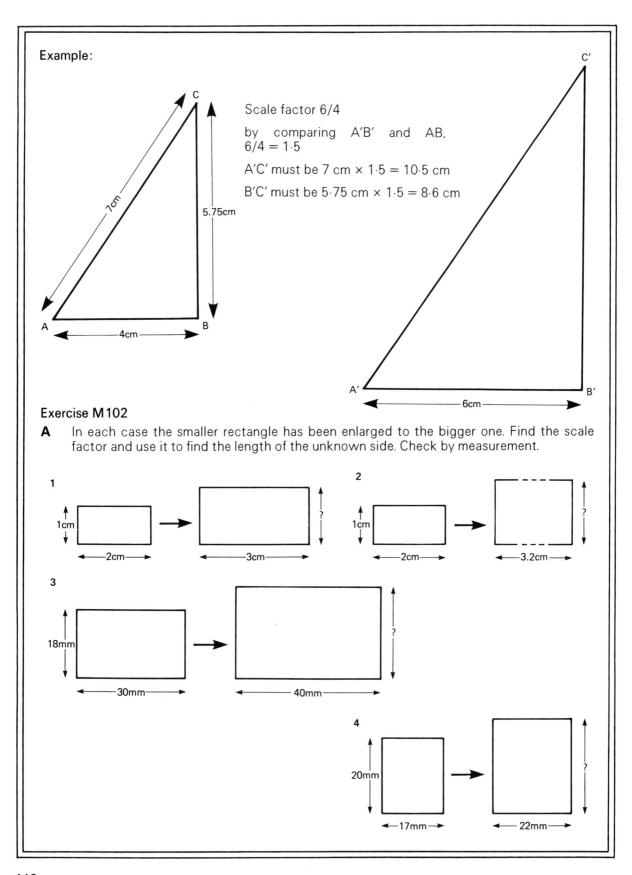

Example:

Scale factor 6/4

by comparing A'B' and AB,
6/4 = 1·5

A'C' must be 7 cm × 1·5 = 10·5 cm

B'C' must be 5·75 cm × 1·5 = 8·6 cm

Exercise M 102

A In each case the smaller rectangle has been enlarged to the bigger one. Find the scale factor and use it to find the length of the unknown side. Check by measurement.

1

2

3

4

5

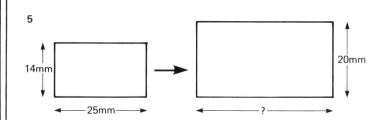

B Check whether the second rectangle is an exact enlargement of the first for these pairs.

Example:

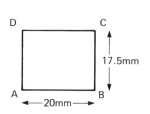 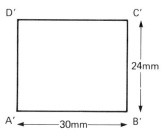

AB → A'B' scale factor 30/20 = 1·5

BC → B'C' scale factor 24/17·5 = 1·37

For an exact enlargement the scale factors should be the same.

So A'B'C'D' is not an exact enlargement of ABCD.

1

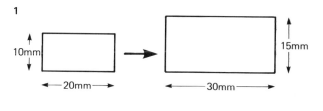

2

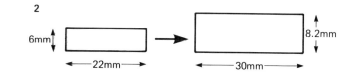

3

4

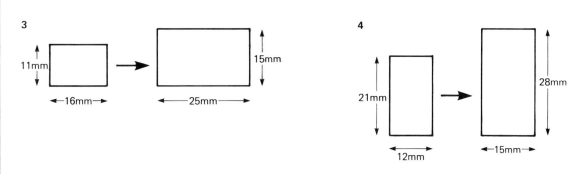

113

5

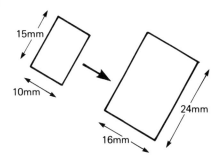

6

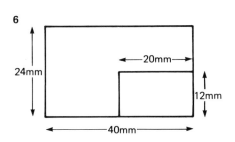

C Rectangles ABCD and A'B'C'D' are drawn. Is A'B'C'D' an exact enlargement of ABCD if:

1 AB = 10 mm   A'B' = 16 mm   **2** AB = 12 mm   A'B' = 15 mm
BC = 18 mm   B'C' = 28·8 mm   BC = 20 mm   B'C' = 25 mm

3 AB = 16 mm   A'B' = 30 mm   **4** AB = 20 mm   A'B' = 42 mm
BC = 25 mm   B'C' = 45 mm   BC = 35 mm   B'C' = 65 mm

Maps and scales

A map is a drawing from which the distance between real places can
be found. You have to know the scale of the map to find these
distances.

Examples:

(a)

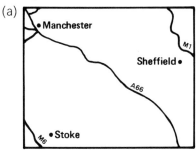

	Distance on map (mm)	True distance (km)
Manchester to Sheffield	40	40
Sheffield to Stoke	41	41
Stoke to Manchester	29	29

Scale   1 : 1 000 000   or   1mm on map ⟷ 1km on ground

NOTE: If the map were enlarged 1 000 000 times
it would fit over the area it shows.

(b) Each mm on the map corresponds to 30 km real distance.

	Distance on map (mm)	True distance (km)
Edinburgh to London	44	660
Edinburgh to Cardiff	40	600
Cardiff to London	17	255

Scale   1:30 000 000   1mm on map ⟷ 30km on ground

Exercise M103

A   These questions refer to the map.

    1   What are the real distances in km between:

        (a) Inverness and Edinburgh
        (b) Perth and Dundee
        (c) Glasgow and Newcastle
        (d) Newcastle and Perth
        (e) Dundee and Glasgow
        (f) Dundee and Inverness

    2   Which is the nearest town on the map to these?

        (a) Perth
        (b) Newcastle
        (c) Dundee
        (d) Inverness

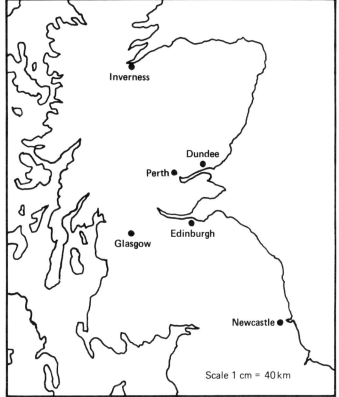

Scale 1 cm = 40 km

B   These maps all have different scales.

1   1 : 20 000 000 1mm ◄──► 20km

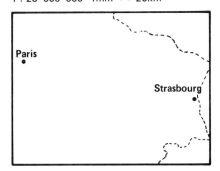

How far from Paris to Strasbourg?

2   1 : 10 000 000 1mm ──── 10km

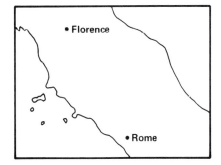

How far from Florence to Rome?

115

3 1 : 150 000 000   1mm ◄──► 150km

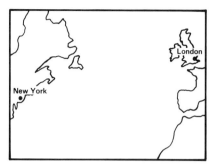

How far from New York to London?

4 1 : 1000 000   1mm ◄──► 1km

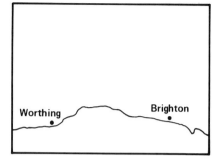

How far from Worthing to Brighton?

5 1 : 100 000 000   1mm ◄──► 100km

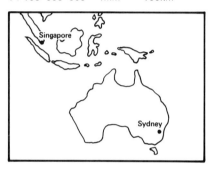

How far from Singapore to Sydney?

6 1 : 250 000 000   1mm ◄──► 250km

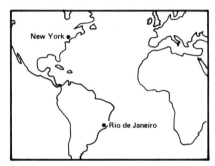

How far from New York to Rio de Janeiro?

C 1

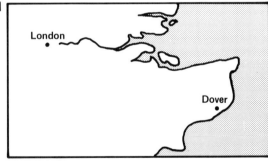

The real distance between London and Dover is 100 km. What is the scale of the map?

2 Fill in the missing parts of this table.

Example:

150 mm → 4500 km
1 mm → 4500/150
→ 30 km
1 mm → 30 000 000 mm
Scale of map 1:30 000 000

Real distance (km)	Map distance (mm)	Scale of map
4500	150	1:30 000 000
300	20	?
175	25	?
600	?	1:10 000 000
800	?	1:20 000 000
50	50	?
?	6	1:5 000 000
?	120	1:1 000 000
?	12	1:100 000

Unit M28   Approximations

Approximate calculations: Estimates

If you use a calculator for arithmetic you have to keep your wits
about you. It is easy to press the wrong button, forget to clear the
machine, or press a button twice and so on.

   Thus for every calculation you should have an estimate ready.
This should not be a longwinded sum or you lose the advantage of
the incredible speed of the machine.

   Here is a suggested routine you could use. Look through it
carefully.

1   Look at the calculation carefully. Can I do it in my head?
    Instantly? (e.g. 75×10, $34/2$, $24/100$)
2   If not, estimate the answer.
    (e.g. $17 \times 23 \rightarrow 20 \times 20 \rightarrow 400$)
3   Calculate on machine.
4   Are the estimate and calculation reasonably close? If yes, then
    finish.
5   If no, repeat calculation carefully, watching the display.
6   Are estimate and calculation reasonably close? If yes, then finish.
7   If no, recheck estimate and calculate by a different method.
8   Are the estimate and machine answer close? If yes, then finish.
9   If no, ask for help from your teacher!

If things go wrong you are probably using the wrong calculator
language or there is something about the calculator that you have
not understood.

Estimating by leading digit approximations

All figures other than the first are treated as zeros in calculating the
estimate.

Examples:

(a) 423×164
     $\downarrow \qquad \downarrow$
     $400 \times 100 \rightarrow 40\,000$

(b) $3854 + 562$
     $\downarrow \qquad \downarrow$
     $3000 + 500 \rightarrow 3500$

(c) $475 \cdot 3 \div 21 \cdot 2$
     $\downarrow \qquad \downarrow$
     $400 \div 20 \rightarrow 20$

Exercise M104

Find leading digit approximations for these calculations. Compare with the actual value given by your calculator.

A
1 $17 + 35$	**2** $86 + 77$	**3** $123 + 95$	**4** $166 + 409$
5 $327 + 580$	**6** $432 + 565$	**7** $934 + 822$	**8** $1436 + 755$
9 $76 - 39$	**10** $80 - 44$	**11** $130 - 79$	**12** $254 - 130$

B
1 14×16	**2** 22×17	**3** 35×46	**4** 66×80
5 135×42	**6** 188×78	**7** $19 \cdot 3 \times 17 \cdot 5$	**8** $4 \cdot 04 \times 5 \cdot 21$
9 $28 \div 16$	**10** $55 \div 12$	**11** $184 \div 26$	**12** $423 \div 66$

Leading digit approximation can be improved by:

1 Rounding up and down   **2** Balancing for $\times$ and $+$.

For subtraction and division both numbers should be increased or decreased.

Examples:

(a) 423×164
$\downarrow\downarrow$
$400 \times 200 \rightarrow 80\,000$

423 is treated as 400 but 164 is taken up to 200.

Thus 423 has been made smaller while 164 has been made larger by 'comparable' amounts.

Leading digit estimate: $40\,000$

Improved estimate: $80\,000$

Exact result (calculator): $69\,372$

Good estimating depends on a 'feel' for the numbers and takes practice. Remember that estimating should be **fast** and **simple**.

(b) $445 - 283$
$\downarrow\downarrow$
$445 - 300 \rightarrow 145$

$445 - 283$
$\downarrow\downarrow$
$465 - 300 \rightarrow 165$

Leaving the first number and changing the second to one that is easy to subtract.

If you wanted to be even closer you could increase the 445 by about the same amount as you increased the 283.

Leading digit estimate: $400 - 200 \rightarrow 200$

Adjusted estimate: $465 - 300 \rightarrow 165$

Exact result (calculator): $445 - 283 \rightarrow 162$

(c) $38 \cdot 2 \div 1 \cdot 45$

Leading digit estimate: $30 \div 1 \rightarrow 30$

Rounded estimate: $40 \div 2 \cdot 0 \rightarrow 20$ (taking both to the nearest easy number above)

Adjusted estimate: $48 \div 2 \rightarrow 24$

Exact result (calculator): $38 \cdot 2 \div 1 \cdot 45 \rightarrow 26 \cdot 34$

($1 \cdot 45$ is increased by about $0 \cdot 5$ to make 2. This is increasing the number by a third of itself. If you now increase $38 \cdot 2$ in roughly the same way you get $38 + 10 = 48$, or more accurately, $38 + 12 = 50$.)

Exercise M105

A Make an estimate for each of these calculations. Try to make the work as simple as possible, but at the same time aim for a close approximation.

Show the steps that lead to your estimate in each case. Compare your estimate with a calculator answer to the problem.

1 $42 + 39$	**2** $463 + 258$	**3** $777 + 1048$	**4** $3648 + 4247$
5 $49 - 32$	**6** $88 - 54$	**7** $236 - 93$	**8** $1400 - 868$
9 36×43	**10** 47×98	**11** 136×49	**12** 363×107
13 $438 \div 22$	**14** $1561 \div 34$	**15** $2923 \div 175$	**16** $4588 \div 226$

B Make an estimate to check these calculations which have been done on a machine. Compare the time it takes to estimate with the time it takes to repeat the calculations on the machine.

1 $54 + 17 = 91$	**2** $137 + 295 = 532$
3 $498 + 755 = 953$	**4** $1457 + 3268 = 5525$
5 $83 - 67 = 16$	**6** $255 - 93 = 162$
7 $744 - 285 = 559$	**8** $2360 - 1299 = 1061$
9 $44 \times 53 = 1832$	**10** $76 \times 87 = 6612$
11 $147 \times 64 = 948$	**12** $232 \times 137 = 31784$
13 $176 \div 19 = 9.26$	**14** $454 \div 23 = 9.74$
15 $788 \div 92 = 7.56$	**16** $5436 \div 135 = 40.27$

C The presence of decimals makes no difference to these methods of estimating although care must be taken in placing the decimal point. This is very often a source of mistakes.

Check these decimal calculations.

1 $3.42 + 6.75 = 10.17$	**2** $2.08 + 11.3 = 133.8$
3 $14.75 + 12.3 = 27.05$	**4** $0.62 + 1.88 = 2.5$
5 $4.00 - 1.76 = 2.24$	**6** $12.60 - 3.08 = 8.98$
7 $1.22 - 0.85 = 0.037$	**8** $0.40 - 0.09 = 0.31$
9 $0.36 \times 0.41 = 1.476$	**10** $2.35 \times 0.24 = 0.564$
11 $1.46 \times 0.08 = 0.1168$	**12** $4.06 \times 3.22 = 1.307$
13 $4.3 \div 1.5 = 2.866$	**14** $1.08 \div 0.25 = 4.32$
15 $3.66 \div 0.48 = 7.625$	**16** $0.38 \div 4.54 = 0.083$

Errors spotted by knowledge of numbers

There are some useful checks which will show up where a mistake has been made.

1 *Odd/even*

We know that:

odd + odd = even	odd × odd = odd
even + even = even	even × even = even
odd + even = odd	odd × even = even

Example:

We can see immediately that 37 + 53 = 91 is incorrect because two odd numbers have been added and the answer should be even.

2 *Table patterns*

A knowledge of the multiplication table up to 10 × 10 allows a check of end figures.

42 × 17 = 716: must be wrong because the answer should end in 4, from 7 × 2 = 14.

66 × 45 = 2970: is likely to be right as it ends in 0, and 5 × 6 = 30 also ends in zero.

3 *Decimal point position*

There is a rule for multiplying decimals that says that there will be the same number of figures after the decimal point both before and after multiplying.

Example:

$0.7 \times 0.4 = 0.28$

↑   ↑   ↑

2 figures after decimal point   *2 figures after decimal point*

This rule does not always hold for the calculator which will show a product like 4·20 as 4·2.

Exercise M 106

A   Use one of the above methods to spot the errors in these calculations.

1	492 + 364 = 856	**2**	525 + 365 = 891
3	1047 + 2139 = 3185	**4**	4·35 + 5·76 = 10·11
5	23 × 37 = 852	**6**	295 × 33 = 9737
7	49 × 78 = 3822	**8**	606 × 44 = 26 666
9	0·3 × 0·2 = 0·6	**10**	0·5 × 0·2 = 1·0
11	4·35 × 0·07 = 0·345	**12**	2·5 × 1·4 = 3·5

B   Carry out the calculations below, taking care to work out the brackets separately.

1	(34 + 17) × 62	**2**	(45 × 16) + 21·4
3	(45/120) + (36/120)	**4**	62 × (12·5 × 38)
5	(513 + 773) + 425	**6**	513 + (773 + 425)
7	12·5 × (38 × 62)	**8**	(245 × 36)/75

C   Carry out the above calculations, but use a different key sequence. Do you still get the same answers?

Unit M29   Tessellations

Tessellations

Some shapes are useful for covering floors, walls, etc. We call this a
tiling or **tessellation**.
   The most commonly used shapes are the square and rectangle.

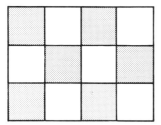

Simple tiling with 1cm
squares in two colours

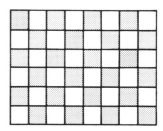

Simple tiling with ½cm
squares in two colours

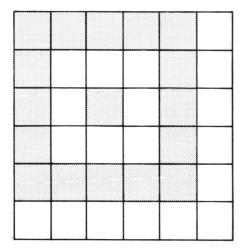

Another tiling with
two colour 1cm squares

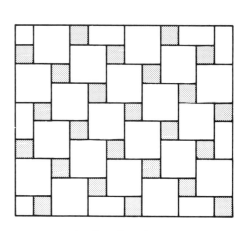

Another tiling with 1cm
and ½cm squares mixed

Exercise M 107

A **1** Design three different tiling patterns using 1 cm square tiles only and two colours. Make your design on squared paper.

2 Design three different tiling patterns using a mixture of 1 cm tiles and $\frac{1}{2}$ cm tiles. Choose your own colours.

3 Design two different tiling patterns using only 2 cm × 1 cm rectangular tiles.

4 Design two different tiling patterns using 2 cm × 1 cm rectangles and 1 cm squares mixed.

B For each of the designs above, estimate the number of white and coloured tiles you would need to cover:

1 100 cm² of floor space

2 250 cm² of floor space

3 1 m² of floor space

4 30 m² of floor space

Do the same for your own designs.

Equilateral triangle

Perfect equilateral triangles can be drawn with compass and ruler.

Example:

To draw an equilateral triangle, side 5 cm

1 Draw a line 5 cm long.

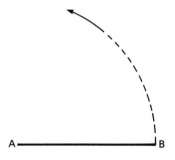

2 With compass point at A, draw an arc of the circle, radius AB.

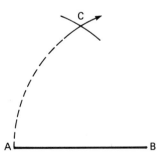

3 With compass point at B, draw an arc of the circle, radius AB.

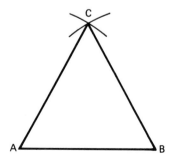

4 Join C to A and B to form the equilateral triangle.

Exercise M108

A Use a pair of compasses and a ruler to draw these figures accurately. They are made up of equilateral triangles.

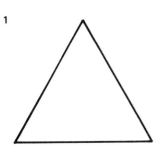

1

Simple equilateral
triangle, side 4·5cm

2

Rhombus
side 4cm

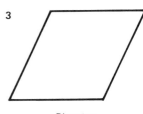

3

Rhombus
side 5cm

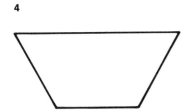

4

Isosceles trapezium
3cm, 3cm, 3cm and 6cm

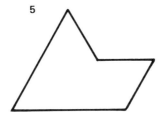

5

Pentagon with sides
4cm, 4cm, 2cm, 2cm and 2cm
The angles are all 60° or 120°

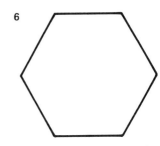

6

The regular hexagon
6 sides, each 2cm long
all angles 120°

B Draw an **isometric grid** on plain paper as follows:

1 Draw a line 150 mm long and mark each 10 mm. Mark this line AB.

2 Draw a line at 60° to the first line and mark it at 10 mm intervals. This angle should be drawn very accurately. Mark a point C, 150 mm from A along this line.

3 Join the interval marks on AB to those on AC.

4 Mark BC at 10 mm intervals and join these marks to those on AC and then AB.

First the space fills with rhombuses and then with equilateral triangles.

You have now formed an isometric grid. The grid may be extended by drawing parallel lines where necessary.

C Use your isometric grid to draw these shapes.

1 An equilateral triangle, side 2 cm.

2 A rhombus of side 3 cm.

3 A regular hexagon, side 1 cm.

4 A regular hexagonal star, side 1 cm.

5 Two different 5-sided figures made up of equilateral triangles.

6 Two different 6-sided figures made up of equilateral triangles.

D   This diagram shows two different tessellation designs on an isometric grid.

Make some designs of your own. (It is possible to buy paper already printed with the grid at an ordinary stationer's shop.)

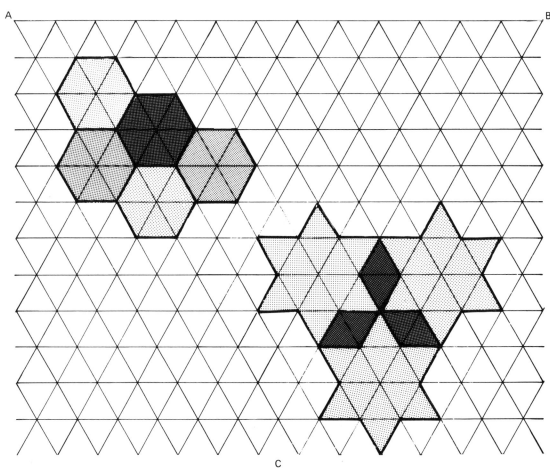

Many geometrical properties of shapes can be seen in a tessellation.

Examples:

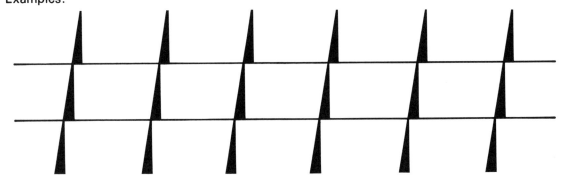

This tessellation shows that a parallelogram covers the same space as a rectangle with the same base and height.

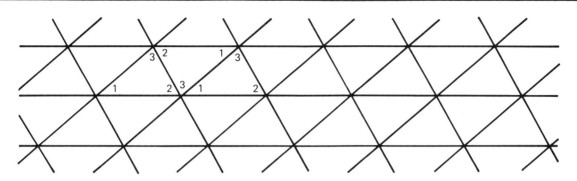

This tessellation shows:

1 The angles of a triangle add to 180°.

2 Three different parallelograms can be made from two congruent triangles.

3 Opposite angles of a parallelogram are equal.

Exercise M109

A Draw any triangle you like on squared paper.

Make a tiling that uses this triangle as the unit. The tiling made only from this triangle can be turned in different ways.

Use the tiling you have made to find:

1 parallelograms

2 trapezia

3 hexagons

4 six-pointed stars.

Show from your tessellation that the three angles of your triangle add to 180°.

B Repeat question **A** but this time start with an isosceles triangle. What differences do you notice in the shapes formed in the tessellation this time?

C Repeat question **A** starting with a right-angled triangle. What changes does this cause in the tessellation and in the shapes of the parallelograms and other figures?

Unit M30   Problem solving III

Related problems

When you have a problem to solve, and you cannot do it, it is a good idea to explore an easier problem which is related to the one you are attempting. If you succeed in solving the easier problem you may use the lessons you have learned to attack the original problem.

The problem

The man in the picture wants a book from the top shelf but has no library steps. He can climb up the shelves, but needs both hands to climb down again, so he cannot carry the book down. He cannot throw the book down or it will be damaged. How can he solve the problem?

The easier problem
How can he get a book which is *just* out of reach?

SOLUTION: He can stand on the bottom shelf, take the book and jump down.

The connecting problem
If he can move the book he wants to a position just out of reach, he can get the book down. He finds that although he cannot climb down with a book in his hand, he can move a book down two shelves providing there is a space free.

Solution to original problem

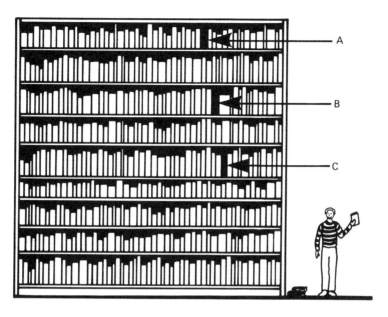

The book he wants is at A.

1 Remove book C, leaving a space.
2 Climb two shelves. Move book B to space C.
3 Climb two shelves. Move book A to space B.
4 Climb down four shelves. Remove book B.
5 Climb up two shelves. Move book A to space C.
6 Climb down two shelves. Remove book A.

Exercise M110

Think about the following problems. In each case find a simpler problem to begin with.

1 Peter cannot swim but he wants to. What should he do?

2 Janet collects wild plants. She wants to **classify** her collection but she does not know what headings to use.

3 Mike wants to make a catalogue of his records. How should he start?

4 Geoff wants to improve his memory. How should he set about it?

5 Liz is training for the high jump during the holidays. What should she do each day?

6 In the bookshelf example before this exercise, how could the librarian put the book back on the top shelf?

Sometimes a problem becomes simpler by choosing a **particular case** to solve.

Examples:

In question **1** above we consider the problem of Peter swimming one width as a start.

In question **5** above we consider Liz trying to jump 1·50 m as a start.

Exercise M111

Think about these problems. Begin by studying a special case.

1 A boy and a girl have one bicycle between them. What is the quickest way they can make a journey? (They cannot both ride the bicycle at the same time.)

2 If you add up the first 100 odd numbers, the answer is 100 × 100. Why is this?

3 If you add up the first 100 even numbers, the answer is (100 × 100) + 100. Why is this?

4

A man has to walk from A to B by straight paths and also has to leave something by the roadside on his way. What is his shortest route?

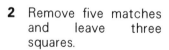

5 A, B and C are beads on parallel wires W_1 and W_2. How would you arrange A, B and C so that the total length AB + BC + CA is as small as possible?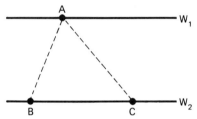

6 George and Linda are arguing. George says that if you throw a number of dice your most likely score is found by multiplying the number of dice you throw by 3. Is he right?

You can learn a lot about your problem-solving skills by making a careful record of how you attempt a puzzle. For each of the puzzles that follow, work with a partner and record all the steps you take to get an answer. Do not worry if you fail to solve a puzzle, put it away and come back to it.

Exercise M112

Match problems

1 Remove two matches and leave two squares.

2 Remove five matches and leave three squares.

3 Remove twelve matches and leave three squares.

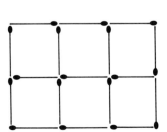

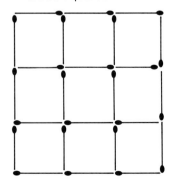

Unit P1

Exercise P1

The addition square is completed by adding across, adding down and then by adding across the bottom totals.

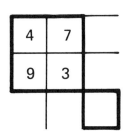
Addition square

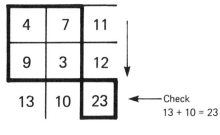
Add across

Add down

←—— Check
13 + 10 = 23

A Complete these addition squares. You should not need the calculator.

1

6	8
9	11

2

7	12
10	14

3

0	9
8	13

4

13	9
18	17

5

19	13
17	14

6

16	18
14	15

7

17	17
15	19

8

19	13
16	17

B Multiplication squares are completed by multiplying instead of adding. Complete these multiplication squares. You should not need the calculator.

1

2	3
4	5

2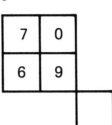

5	6
3	8

3

7	0
6	9

4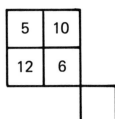

5	10
12	6

5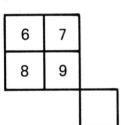

6	7
8	9

6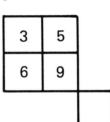

3	5
6	9

7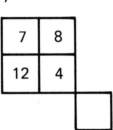

7	8
12	4

8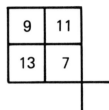

9	11
13	7

Exercise P2

A Complete the × 7 table up to 7 × 10.

×	1	2	3	4	...
7	7	14	21	28	...

Use your table to work out these multiplications and divisions.

1 7 × 5	**2** 7 × 7	**3** 7 × 10	**4** 9 × 7	**5** 6 × 7
6 8 × 7	**7** 35 ÷ 7	**8** 49 ÷ 7	**9** 28 ÷ 7	**10** 56 ÷ 7
11 70 ÷ 7	**12** 63 ÷ 7	**13** 42 ÷ 7	**14** 7 × 12	**15** 7 × 14
16 84 ÷ 7	**17** 105 ÷ 7	**18** 98 ÷ 7	**19** 140 ÷ 7	**20** 280 ÷ 7

B Complete the × 9 table up to 9 × 10.

×	1	2	3	4	...
9	9	18	27	36	...

Use your table to work out these multiplications and divisions.

1 4 × 9	**2** 9 × 5	**3** 6 × 9	**4** 8 × 9	**5** 9 × 10
6 9 × 9	**7** 45 ÷ 9	**8** 36 ÷ 9	**9** 54 ÷ 9	**10** 27 ÷ 9
11 63 ÷ 9	**12** 81 ÷ 9	**13** 99 ÷ 9	**14** 9 × 12	**15** 9 × 15
16 9 × 20	**17** 135 ÷ 9	**18** 162 ÷ 9	**19** 108 ÷ 9	**20** 180 ÷ 9

Exercise P3

A Write down the buttons you would press to obtain these numbers on the display of your calculator.

1 *22*   **2** *333*   **3** *4567*   **4** *13500*

5 *202*   **6** *666333*   **7** *50000*   **8** *121212*

B Follow these sequences. What would you expect to see on the display at the end? Check that you are right.

1 C 2 3 0 5   **2** C 0 0 5 4   **3** C 5 0 4 0

4 C 7 7 7 7   **5** C 0 7 0 7   **6** C 0 6 0 9 0

C Pick out the errors in these.

Key sequence	Display
C 0 6 6 6 6	*66660*
C 3 4 4 3 5	*3435*
C 2 0 8 8 4	*20884*
C 3 6 9 1 3	*369113*
C 2 7 8 3 2 5	*278235*

D A calculator was put together wrongly. It showed all the numbers in 'mirror writing'. What should have been seen when this calculator showed:

1    **2**    **3**

4    **5**

6

Unit P2

Exercise P4

A Use the calculator to complete these addition squares.

1
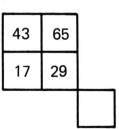

2
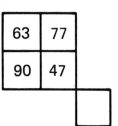

3
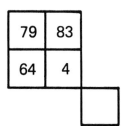

4
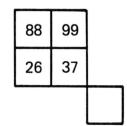

5
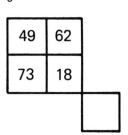

6
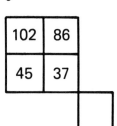

7
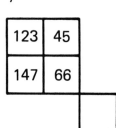

8
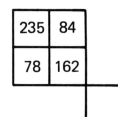

Note: There is no need to estimate these as the sums are self-checking.

B Use the calculator to add these.

1	48	**2**	39	**3**	67	**4**	77	**5**	93	**6**	72
	73		59		75		88		87		29
	29		8		32		99		67		39

7	153	**8**	256	**9**	362	**10**	123	**11**	284	**12**	373
	76		145		8		77		683		419
	84		99		445		289		179		665

13	48	**14**	59	**15**	147	**16**	299	**17**	365	**18**	218
	9		66		69		356		429		96
	92		75		208		144		713		7
	77		88		79		75		888		432

Exercise P5

A   Use the calculator to subtract these. Guess first.

1 100 − 45   **2** 100 − 66   **3** 100 − 91   **4** 100 − 7

5 100 − 36   **6** 100 − 18   **7** 100 − 77   **8** 100 − 62

B   Use your calculator to find the errors in this collection of subtractions.

1	**2**	**3**	**4**	**5**	**6**
600	350	477	285	793	604
−415	−127	−128	−196	−186	−288
185	233	251	99	607	316

7	**8**	**9**	**10**	**11**	**12**
255	300	999	805	385	868
− 89	−177	−263	−177	−199	−686
146	233	736	628	214	182

C   Subtract these with pencil and paper. Use your calculator to check your answer.

1	**2**	**3**	**4**	**5**	**6**
88	96	89	90	80	70
−37	−23	−26	−45	−36	−49

7	**8**	**9**	**10**	**11**	**12**
18	36	45	61	73	94
− 9	−17	−27	−28	−37	−58

Exercise P6

A   If you subtract 3 − 9 on the calculator you get the result −6. If you add 6 you get the result 0.

[C] [3] [−] [9] [=] [+] [6] [=]
 0   3   3   9 −6 −6   6   0

1   Write down five different ways of getting −7 on the display.

Write down what you would expect to see on the display for each of these sequences. Check on your calculator.

2 [C] [8] [−] [1] [2] [=]   **3** [C] [6] [−] [9] [=]

4 [C] [4] [−] [1] [0] [=]   **5** [C] [0] [−] [5] [=]

6 [C] [0] [−] [8] [=]   **7** [C] [0] [−] [2] [7] [=]

8 [C] [3] [−] [5] [+] [2]   **9** [C] [0] [−] [4] [+] [4] [=]

10 [C] [0] [−] [8] [+] [8] [=]

B   **1**   You have seen that −6 + 6 = 0. What would you expect −6 + 8 to be equal to?

Write down what you would expect to see on the display for each of these sequences. Check on the machine. It is important that you write them out before pressing the buttons!

2 [C] [0] [−] [6] [+] [8] [=]   **3** [C] [0] [−] [7] [+] [9] [=]

4 [C] [0] [−] [5] [+] [9] [=]   **5** [C] [0] [−] [8] [+] [1] [2] [=]

6 [C] [0] [−] [7] [+] [3] [=]   **7** [C] [0] [−] [5] [+] [2] [=]

8 [C] [0] [−] [9] [+] [6] [=]

Unit P3

Exercise P7

A Measure these straight lines in mm. If they were joined in one long line, would they stretch 50 cm?

1 2 3 4 5 6 7 8 9 10 11 12 13

B Measure the **diagonals*** of these rectangles in mm. What do you notice about the two diagonals of each rectangle?

1   2   3   4   5

*Diagonals are lines joining opposite corners of the rectangle.

C Measure the **diameters*** of these circles. What do you notice about the diameters of each circle?

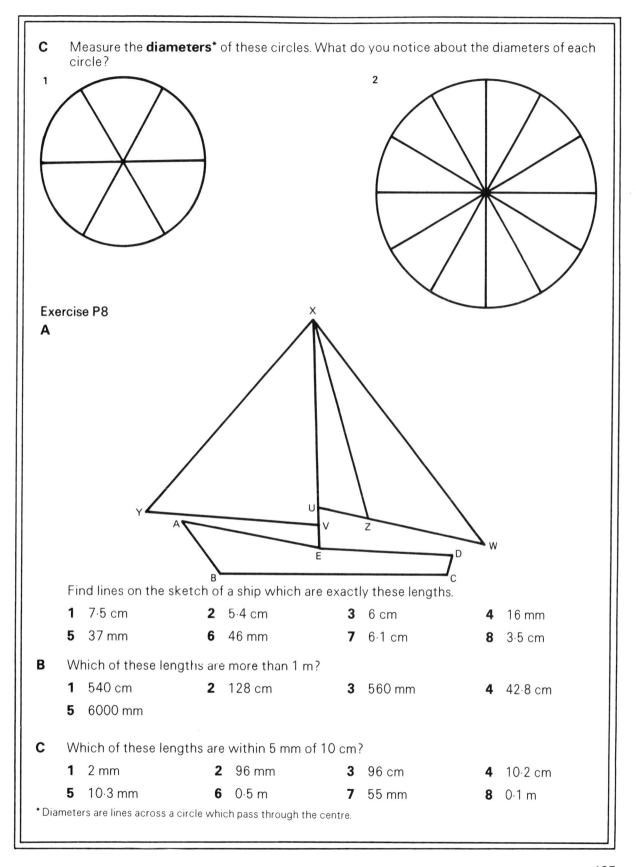

1

2

Exercise P8

A

Find lines on the sketch of a ship which are exactly these lengths.

1 7·5 cm	**2** 5·4 cm	**3** 6 cm	**4** 16 mm
5 37 mm	**6** 46 mm	**7** 6·1 cm	**8** 3·5 cm

B Which of these lengths are more than 1 m?

1 540 cm	**2** 128 cm	**3** 560 mm	**4** 42·8 cm
5 6000 mm			

C Which of these lengths are within 5 mm of 10 cm?

1 2 mm	**2** 96 mm	**3** 96 cm	**4** 10·2 cm
5 10·3 mm	**6** 0·5 m	**7** 55 mm	**8** 0·1 m

*Diameters are lines across a circle which pass through the centre.

135

Exercise P9

A   Estimate these measurements.

     1   How many g of food do you eat in a day?

     2   How many g of liquid do you drink in a day?

     3   How many mm do you grow in a month?

     4   How much does a bicycle weigh in kg?

     5   How far do you walk to school in a day? How far in a week?

     6   How long is your longest hair?

     7   How much does a newly born kitten weigh?

     8   How much does a kite weigh?

B   Follow these instructions on mm² graph paper.

     1   Start near the left-hand side.
         Draw a line XY 3 cm long, turn left.
         Draw a line YZ 30 mm long, turn right.
         Draw ZA 15 mm long, turn right.
         Draw AB 5 cm long, turn right.
         Draw BC 3·7 cm long, turn right.
         Draw CD 20 mm long.

         How far is D straight from X?

     2   Start 4 cm in from the top left-hand side.

         Draw AB straight down 8·0 cm, turn left.
         Draw BC 10 mm, turn left.
         Draw CD 48 mm, turn right.
         Draw DE 1 cm, turn right.
         Draw EF 60 mm, turn left.
         Draw FG 1·5 cm, turn left.
         Draw GH 7·2 cm, turn right.
         Draw HI 17 mm, turn right.
         Draw IJ 80 mm, turn right.
         Draw JK 7·2 cm, turn right.
         Draw KL 10 cm, turn right.
         Draw LM 20 mm.

         (a)   Which lines go up and down the graph paper?
         (b)   Which lines go across the graph paper?
         (c)   Compare the number of right turns with the number of left turns.
         (d)   What do you notice about the points A and M?

Unit P4

Exercise P 10

Liquids are always being measured for different reasons. We put milk into pint and litre bottles; oil into pint, litre and gallon cans; perfume into 5 ml, 10 ml bottles; medicine into 5 ml, 10 ml spoons, 50 ml, 100 ml bottles, and so on.

A   **1** Keep a notebook of all the different ways of measuring liquids that you see in shops, home or school or anywhere else.

      2 Put these quantities in order of size, largest first.
          1 litre, 1 pint, 2 pints, 6 ml, 1 gallon, 5 litres, 10 cl, $\frac{1}{2}$ litre, 200 ml, $\frac{1}{2}$ pint, 50 cl.

      3 How many centilitres of liquid would you expect these to hold?

          (a) an empty can of baked beans   (b) a 1 litre bottle
          (c) a hot water bottle   (d) a wine glass
          (e) a teacup   (f) a teapot

B   Liz found three empty bottles, 1 litre, $\frac{1}{2}$ litre and 200 ml. She decided to use them to **calibrate** the litre bottle, that is to mark the bottle so that she could measure liquid in it. She had a jug of water, an indelible* pencil and a funnel, so that she could pour from one bottle to another without losing any liquid.

How did she manage to mark the litre bottle at every 100 ml?

Exercise P 11

A   *A day in the life of Metric Mary*
All the quantities in this story are wrong. Choose reasonable quantities to replace the ones given in the story, and give a reason for your choice each time.

One morning Mary got up at 9 pm. She had a bath in 5 litres of water, carefully adding 20 litres of bath scent. She cleaned her teeth and drank 1 ml of water. For breakfast she had some orange juice (5 ml), an egg, toast (5 g) and a cup of delicious coffee (20 ml).

Next, Mary went out shopping, she paid £4·75 on the bus journey which took 7 hrs 52 minutes. When she got to town she bought 20 kg of potatoes, a loaf of bread (5 kg), a bottle of lemonade (50 ml), a cabbage (50 g), a lettuce (2 kg) and 6 kg of biscuits. She also bought a 5 litre tin of polish and 5 litres of washing up liquid. On the way back to the bus she bought 5 cm of material to make a skirt and 2500 buttons for her sister.

*One that makes a mark that cannot be rubbed out.

B Remember to put every measure in the same units before adding or subtracting. Work out these.

1	5 kg + 500 g	**2**	0·6 m + 45 cm	**3**	£0·06 + 70p
4	5 cl + 35 ml	**5**	35 mm + 6 cm	**6**	250 cm + 4·5 m
7	350 ml + 0·55 litre	**8**	£1·45 + 35p	**9**	4 kg − 300 g
10	1 m − 75 cm	**11**	£6·30 − 140p	**12**	10 cl − 55 ml
13	6 cm − 15 mm	**14**	2 m − 45 cm	**15**	2·5 litres − 350 ml
16	£4·20 − 108p				

Exercise P 12

A Work out the cost of each of the following. Look carefully at the units, and the cost per unit.

1	4 litres of oil at £1·20 a litre	**2**	20 metres of wood at 20p a metre
3	5 kg of potatoes at 16p per kg	**4**	50 g of ointment at 70p per 100 g
5	500 g of butter at 80p per kg	**6**	5 litres of petrol at 30p per litre
7	2 metres of cloth at £1·75 a metre	**8**	10 cl of perfume at 65p per cl
9	3 kg of meat at £2·20 per kg	**10**	20 cm of silver wire at 12p per cm
11	400 g of cheese at £1 per kilo	**12**	50 cl of spirit at £3 per litre
13	10 g of gold at £700 per kg	**14**	2 litres of medicine at 5p per cl
15	400 g of ham at 80p per 100 g	**16**	600 g of sausages at £2 per kilo
17	50 cm of lace at £1·40 per m	**18**	100 m of kite string at £1 per 50 m
19	3 kilos of sauce at 20p per 100 g	**20**	2 kilos of syrup at 80p per 400 g

B Which of these pairs is better value for money?

1 2 kg of soap powder for £1·50 *or* 500 g of the same for 40p.

2 70p for 70 cm of wood *or* £8 for 10 m of the same wood.

3 100 g of salt for 65p *or* 1 kg of salt for £3·50.

4 6 metres of carpet for £75 *or* 1 metre of carpet for £7·50.

5 2 litres of paint for £4·50 *or* 5 litres of paint for £10.

6 1 litre of paint stripper for £1·80 *or* 200 cl of the same for 75p.

7 2 litres of wine for £3·80 *or* 1 bottle (700 ml) for £1·40.

8 50 cm of ribbon for 60p *or* 2 m of ribbon for £2·50.

9 10 m of sticky tape for 50p *or* 25 m of sticky tape for £1.

10 1 kg of nails for £1·20 *or* 100 g of nails for 25p.

Unit P5

Exercise P13

Since the calculator does multiplication, cost problems become very easy.

Example:

Find the cost of 16 light bulbs at 27p each.

16 × 27p = 432p = £4·32   (by calculator)

Answer: The light bulbs cost £4·32

Estimate: 20 × 20p = 400p = £4

A   Find the cost of:

1   12 teeshirts at 74p each
2   16 oranges at 7p each
3   23 teapots at 84p each
4   75 spoons at 13p each
5   27 towels at £1·45 each
6   42 pairs of socks at 66p each
7   48 pillowcases at 76p each
8   55 fish-hooks at $7\frac{1}{2}$p each

B   Would a £10 note be enough to buy these? Guess first.

1   36 packets of seed at 26p a packet.
2   24 bottles of oil at 37p a bottle.
3   25 rose bushes at 48p a bush.
4 $12\frac{1}{2}$ tickets to a match at 75p a ticket.
5   37 packets of crisps at 33p a packet.
6   48 bars of chocolate at 22p a bar.

C   Work out this bill on your calculator to check it. If you find mistakes, put them right and work out a new correct total.

	£	p
3 lbs of meat at £1·24 a lb	3	75
3 doz eggs at 74p a doz	2	32
4 bottles of mayonnaise at 72p each	2	98
6 tins of soup at 28p a tin	1	78
5 oranges at $10\frac{1}{2}$p each		$62\frac{1}{2}$
12 packets of crisps at 33p a packet	3	99
2 bottles of wine at £2·35 a bottle	4	70
5 packets of biscuits at 35p a packet	2	10
Total	84	12

Exercise P 14

Multiplying weights and measures is just the same as multiplying numbers. You may wish to alter the units at the end of the calculation. Make a rough estimate each time. Present your answer in a sentence.

Example:

Find the weight of 45 tins of spaghetti if one tin weighs 454 g.

45 × 454 g = 20 430 g
= 20·43 kg (changing the units from g to kg)

Answer: The 45 tins would weigh 20·43 kg

Check: 45 × 450 g is nearly the same as 40 × 500 g = 20 000 g = 20 kg

A   **1**   A bottle of milk weighs 667 g including the bottle. What does a crate of 24 bottles weigh if the crate weighs 1000 g?

2   A milk float carries 84 crates, each with 24 bottles of milk. Is this more than 1 tonne (1000 kg)?

3   A lorry carries 250 crates of milk each with 24 bottles. What is the load on the lorry?

4   Potatoes are loaded in 56 lb bags in the country. A lorry brings 420 bags to London. How many pounds of potatoes in this load? If 100 lb = 45 kg, how many kg of potatoes are there in the load?

5   A car transporter carries 8 cars, each one weighing 1160 kg. What does the load weigh?

B   **1**   A brick has a height of 12 cm. What is the height of a wall 28 bricks high if the mortar is 1 cm thick?

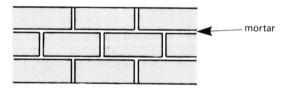

2   Fencing is made in units of 150 cm length. How long is a fence which is made up of 48 such units?

3   A cotton reel contains 94½ m of thread. What length of thread is there on 12 such reels?

4   A bottle of red wine holds 70 cl of wine. Could you fill 36 bottles from a cask holding 24 litres of wine?

5   A milk lorry carries 12 000 litres of milk. Will this supply the 4625 households of a town, if the average household takes about 2½ litres of milk?

C   **1**   A farmer takes 24 sheep to market. He hopes to sell them for at least £35 each. How much cash does he hope to take altogether?

2   Cloth costs £1·45 a metre. What would be the cost of the following lengths?

(a) 3 metres   (b) 12 metres   (c) 25 metres   (d) 75 metres

3   Plywood is sold for £6·80 per m². What would 25 m² cost?

4 When cocoa was worth £1614 per tonne, what would have been the value of a cargo of 2500 tonnes?

5 Some carpet costs £5·75 a square metre. What would the cost be of (a) 12 m², (b) 18 m², (c) 25 m² of this carpet?

6 When a new school is built the cost can be worked out per m² of floor space. If each pupil needs $2\frac{1}{2}$ m² of space:

(a) How much space is needed for a school of 1200 pupils?
(b) How much will the school cost to build at £450 per m².

Unit P6

Exercise P 15

A   Use your calculator to find the results of these divisions.
Note: When using a calculator you should always expect to get all the answers correct. It takes so little time to check, by multiplying back, or to repeat the division. You should also present your work very carefully so that it can be read easily and looks nice.

1 8 ÷ 5	**2** 12 ÷ 6	**3** 18 ÷ 4	**4** 24 ÷ 5	**5** 22 ÷ 3
6 28 ÷ 7	**7** 32 ÷ 8	**8** 45 ÷ 7	**9** 42 ÷ 7	**10** 51 ÷ 3
11 46 ÷ 4	**12** 48 ÷ 4	**13** 50 ÷ 6	**14** 55 ÷ 5	**15** 58 ÷ 7
16 63 ÷ 9	**17** 66 ÷ 8	**18** 74 ÷ 9	**19** 87 ÷ 5	**20** 91 ÷ 7

Add up all your answers. If you have made no mistakes the answer should come to 162·65.

B   Dividing units of measurement in metric is just the same as dividing numbers. You might decide to change the units after division.

Example:

1 m ÷ 8 = 0·125 m *or* 12·5 cm

1 8·0 m ÷ 12	**2** 3·5 m ÷ 7	**3** 14 cm ÷ 12	**4** 28 cm ÷ 7
5 5 kg ÷ 24	**6** 10 kg ÷ 20	**7** 250 g ÷ 8	**8** 400 g ÷ 15
9 5 litres ÷ 20	**10** 65 litres ÷ 18	**11** 22 cl ÷ 3	**12** 15 ml ÷ 8
13 £42 ÷ 36	**14** £8·50 ÷ 14	**15** £3·45 ÷ 7	**16** 95p ÷ 11

C   Word problems

Use your calculator, but make a rough guess first.

1   A painter uses 12 litres of paint to paint 20 m of fence. How much paint is this per metre of fence?

2   A boy buys 24 fireworks for £3·50. How much does each firework cost?

3   A car travels 325 km on 14 gallons of petrol. How far does it travel per gallon? If 1 gallon = 4·5 litres, how far does the car travel on one litre of petrol?

4   10 kg of apples cost £2·50. (a) How much do the apples cost per kg? (b) What weight of apples could I buy for £1?

5   A piece of wood 12 metres long is cut into 16 equal parts. How long is each part?

6   A space ship travelling at 12 500 km per hour is travelling from the earth to the moon. How long will it take to get there? (The moon is approximately 400 000 km from the earth.)

142

7 A girl buys a racing bike by paying 1/24th of the cost each month for two years. If the cost is £84·50, how much does she pay each month?

8 A farmer collects 650 litres of milk each day from his cows. He puts the milk into 45 litre milk churns. How many churns will be collected by the milk lorry each day?

Exercise P 16

Division and multiplication

The question 'What × 6 = 18?' is answered by 18 ÷ 6 = 3
and 'what ÷ 5 = 20?' is answered by 20 × 5 = 100.

A Find the correct numbers to replace the question marks.

1 ? × 4 = 20	**2** ? × 3 = 16	**3** ? × 7 = 25	**4** ? × 6 = 44
5 ? × 12 = 49	**6** 8 × ? = 36	**7** 21 × ? = 44	**8** 16 × ? = 80
9 ? ÷ 3 = 27	**10** ? ÷ 5 = 42	**11** ? ÷ 6 = 72	**12** ? ÷ 9 = 23
13 44 ÷ ? = 11	**14** 56 ÷ ? = 24	**15** 100 ÷ ? = 40	**16** 120 ÷ ? = 65

B 5 × 4 = 20 is the same as these statements:

20 ÷ 5 = 4   20 ÷ 4 = 5   4 × 5 = 20

Write down the three statements which are the same as:

1 4 × 6 = 24	**2** 5 × 8 = 40	**3** 7 × 9 = 63	**4** 8 × 11 = 88
5 84 ÷ 7 = 12	**6** 96 ÷ 12 = 8	**7** 75 ÷ 3 = 25	**8** 141 ÷ 3 = 47

Use the following facts to answer the questions below. Check on the calculator after you have found the answers.

Facts:
4 × 15 = 60   5 × 35 = 175   22 × 17 = 374
117 ÷ 9 = 13   45 ÷ 15 = 3   108 ÷ 18 = 6

Questions:

1 175 ÷ 5 = ?	**2** 3 × 15 = ?	**3** 175 × 35 = ?	**4** 60 ÷ 4 = ?
5 117 ÷ 13 = ?	**6** 374 ÷ 22 = ?	**7** 6 × 18 = ?	**8** 9 × 13 = ?
9 18 × 6 = ?	**10** 9 × ? = 117	**11** 17 × ? = 374	**12** 60 ÷ 15 = ?
13 ? ÷ 17 = 22	**14** ? ÷ 4 = 15	**15** ? × 15 = 45	**16** 5 × ? = 175

C Each of these questions is the same as:

? times something = something else
or ? divided by something = something else

Find the answer to each question and explain the calculation you use.

1 Mr X bought 5 kg of apples for 75p. What did each kilogram cost?

2 Mr Y shared some cheese between 6 people. Each person had 23 g. How much cheese was shared?

3 After an accident there were 14 people in a lifeboat. The captain allowed 75 ml of water per person per day from a supply of 100 litres. How long would the water supply last?

Unit P7

A Find all the factors you can for each of these numbers.

1 10	**2** 15	**3** 21	**4** 27	**5** 36	**6** 40
7 43	**8** 54	**9** 60	**10** 65	**11** 72	**12** 80

B 43 will not divide by 1, 2, 3 or 5 and so it must be prime. Follow these reasons carefully.

1 4 cannot be a factor because 2 is not a factor.

2 6 cannot be a factor because 2 is not a factor (nor is 3).

3 If one of the factors was bigger than 6 then the other factor which produced 43 would be smaller than 6 and we already have shown that there are no factors smaller than 6.

Use similar arguments to show that these numbers are prime:

67, 83, 97

C Write out all the numbers from 1 to 20 in a line.

1 Cross out every 2nd number except 2.

2 Then cross out every 3rd number except 3.

3 Put rings round the numbers that are left. What do you notice about this collection of numbers?

4 Extend your set of numbers up to 50. This time cross out every 2nd, 3rd, 5th and 7th number except the first ones. What can you say about the numbers that are left?

5 Use this method to find all the prime numbers up to 100. The method is called the Sieve of Eratosthenes. He lived more than 2000 years ago.

Prime factors

These are factors of a number that are also prime.

Examples:

Prime factors of 10 are 5 and 2. Both 5 and 2 are prime numbers.

Prime factors of 12 are 2 and 3. 4 and 6 are not primes though both are factors of 12.

Exercise P 18

A Write down the prime factors of these numbers.

1 8	**2** 18	**3** 25	**4** 27	**5** 36	**6** 40
7 45	**8** 48	**9** 50	**10** 60	**11** 66	**12** 75

B Every number can be written as the product of primes.

Examples:

$20 = 5 \times 4 = 5 \times 2 \times 2 = 5 \times 2^2$

Note: We write 2×2 as 2^2

$36 = 9 \times 4 = 3 \times 3 \times 2 \times 2 = 3^2 \times 2^2$

Write these numbers as the product of primes.

1 9	**2** 12	**3** 18	**4** 20	**5** 24	**6** 28
7 30	**8** 32	**9** 36	**10** 42	**11** 48	**12** 56

C *Dividing out the primes*

If we want to express a larger number as the product of primes, we use a system.

Example:

Express 420 as a product of primes.

2	420	divide by 2
2	210	divide by 2
3	105	2 will not divide again so divide by 3 if possible (the next prime)
5	35	3 will not divide again so divide by 5 if possible (the next prime)
	7	7 is a prime itself so we stop the process.

Answer: $420 = 7 \times 5 \times 3 \times 2 \times 2 = 7 \times 5 \times 3 \times 2^2$

Express these numbers as the product of primes.

1 48	**2** 60	**3** 180	**4** 72
5 210	**6** 270	**7** 322	**8** 660

Exercise P 19

You can use your calculator to check for primes.

A Make a list of all the prime numbers up to 97 (see Exercise P17 **C5** above).

B Use your list of prime numbers to test the following numbers to see if they are primes. As soon as the result of dividing by a test prime is smaller than the prime itself, you can stop.

Example:

To test 197

	$197 \div 2$	not necessary because 197 is odd
(next prime)	$197 \div 3$	not necessary because $1 + 9 + 7$ is not a multiple of 3
(next prime)	$197 \div 5$	not necessary because 197 does not end in 0 or 5
(next prime)	$197 \div 7$	$= 28.142$, so 197 does not divide exactly by 7
(next prime)	$197 \div 11$	$= 17.909$, so 197 does not divide exactly by 11
(next prime)	$197 \div 13$	$= 15.153$, so 197 does not divide exactly by 13
(next prime)	$197 \div 17$	$= 11.588$, no need to go any further because 11 is less than 17

so 197 is a prime number.

Remember: A number is prime if no other number will divide into it without leaving a remainder, *or* whatever you divide by, there is always a remainder. (Not counting the number itself.)

1	477	**2**	557	**3**	795	**4**	913	**5**	981	**6**	1253
7	2627	**8**	3313	**9**	4027	**10**	1849	**11**	1363	**12**	5893

Unit P8

Exercise P20

A **1** Write these numbers in standard form.

(a) 4000   (b) 90 000   (c) 240   (d) 3600

(e) 495   (f) 5820   (g) 65 500   (h) 712 000

2 Write these standard form numbers out in full.

(a) 6×10^3 (b) 4.3×10^4 (c) 2.5×10^1 (d) 3.5×10^6

(e) 1.52×10^2 (f) 3.66×10^4 (g) 9.15×10^1 (h) 7.36×10^6

Check using calculator.

B Rewrite this information using standard for the numbers.

1 In 1973, 14 000 000 families owned 3 000 000 cars. By 1979 13 500 000 families owned 5 500 000 cars.

2 The population of Nigeria is between 75 and 80 million people.

3 A modern telescope has 500 000 times the power of the human eye.

4 The diameter of the sun is 864 000 miles and the sun is 13 000 000 times the size of the earth (by volume).

5 In every drop of water there are more than 100 000 000 000 000 000 000 molecules.

6 Germs are so small that if you put 10 000 of them end to end they would only measure 1 cm together.

C Write the standard form numbers out in full from this information.

1 The human body may contain 1×10^{10} nerve cells.

2 The distance from earth to sun is 1.49×10^8 km.

3 The distance from earth to the nearest star is 3.96×10^{13} km.

4 The population of Great Britain is 5.6×10^7.

5 The population of the USA is about 2.4×10^8.

Exercise P21

Multiplication using standard form numbers

Where numbers are very large it is often helpful to use standard form. This avoids mistakes.

Examples: $2000 \times 300 \rightarrow 600\,000$

$2 \times 10^3 \times 3 \times 10^2 \rightarrow 6 \times 10^5$

$(8 \times 10^2) \times (4 \times 10^3) \rightarrow 32 \times 10^2 \times 10^3 \rightarrow 32 \times 10^5 \rightarrow 3 \cdot 2 \times 10^6$

$800 \times 4000 \rightarrow 3\,200\,000$

A Work out these multiplications. Change to standard form first and check on the calculator.

1 3000×300 **2** $20\,000 \times 400$ **3** 3000×1400

4 $5000 \times 500\,000$ **5** 6000×7000 **6** $7000 \times 80\,000$

7 $24\,000 \times 360\,000$ **8** $420\,000 \times 61\,000\,000$ **9** $3300 \times 45\,000\,000$

Note: To multiply decimals on the calculator, use the decimal point key to set in the number. For example, $4 \cdot 2$ will use keys ④ ⊡ ②.

B **1** Find the squares of these numbers.

    (a) 2×10^3 (b) 5×10^4 (c) 8×10^5 (d) 9×10^7

    (e) $1 \cdot 2 \times 10^4$ (f) $2 \cdot 5 \times 10^3$ (g) $1 \cdot 3 \times 10^2$ (h) $4 \cdot 4 \times 10^5$

2 Find the cubes of these numbers.

n cubed $= 1 \times n \times n \times n = n^3$. Write your answer in standard form each time.

    (a) 20   (b) 8   (c) 16   (d) 30   (e) 60

    (f) 75   (g) 95   (h) 170   (i) 200   (j) 640

3 Show that the cube of 2×10 is the same as (the cube of 2) $\times$ (the cube of 10) and work out the cubes of the following.

    (a) 5×10 (b) 3×10^2 (c) 4×10^3 (d) 5×10^4

    Write the result in standard form each time.

C Estimate which of the following pairs of numbers is the larger.

1 $3 \cdot 4 \times 10^7$ *or* $1 \cdot 3 \times 10^8$

2 $(2 \times 10^3) \times (3 \times 10^4)$ *or* 5×10^7

3 $(4 \times 10^3) \times (5 \times 10^3)$ *or* 7×10^9

4 $(2 \cdot 3 \times 10^2) \times (3 \cdot 4 \times 10^3)$ *or* $(8 \cdot 2 \times 10^2) \times (6 \cdot 5 \times 10^2)$

5 $(4 \cdot 5 \times 10^6) \times (3 \times 10^3)$ *or* $(1 \cdot 5 \times 10^4) \times (2 \times 10^5)$

Warning: Numbers in standard form must have the same power of 10 before you can add or subtract them.

Example: $(2 \times 10^2) + (3 \times 10^3)$

$(2 \times 10^2) + (30 \times 10^2) \rightarrow 32 \times 10^2$

D Work out these with care. Check by changing to fully written numbers.

1 $(3 \times 10^3) + (4 \times 10^2)$ **2** $(5 \times 10^2) + (4 \times 10^1)$ **3** $(4 \times 10^3) + (6 \times 10^6)$

4 $(5 \times 10^4) + (8 \times 10^3)$ **5** $(3 \times 10^6) + (4 \times 10^4)$ **6** $(9 \times 10^3) + (9 \times 10^7)$

Unit P9

Exercise P22

A Explain the rotations and translations that are taking place when:

    1 You are riding along a straight road on a bicycle.

    2 You are mixing food with a mixer.

    3 A lorry is driving along with ready-mix concrete.

    4 A tip-up lorry is delivering some sand.

    5 You are swimming doing the front crawl.

B You will need a piece of tracing paper and mm² graph paper and a drawing pin.

    Copy the flag on to graph paper. Use the tracing paper to work out where the flag could be after:

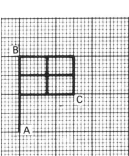

    1 a rotation of 90°, keeping point A fixed with the drawing pin

    2 a rotation of 180°, keeping point A fixed with the pin

    3 a rotation of 90°, keeping point B fixed with the pin

    4 a rotation of 90°, keeping point C fixed with the pin

    5 a translation of 2 cm to the right →

    6 a translation of 3 cm down ↓

    7 a translation of 4 cm up ↑

    8 a translation of 1 cm to the left ←

C Work out the final position of the flag after each of these combinations of rotation and translation.

    1 A translation of 3 cm to the right and then a rotation of 90°.

    2 A translation of 2 cm up and then a rotation of 180°.

3 A rotation of 90° and then a translation of 3 cm to the right.

4 A rotation of 180° and then a translation of 2 cm up.

Exercise P23

A **1** Measure the angles marked in each of the figures.

(a) 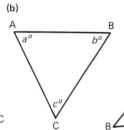 (b) 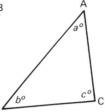 (c) 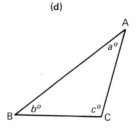 (d) 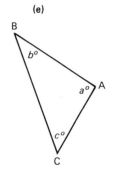 (e)

2 Calculate $a° + b° + c°$ for each triangle.

3 Measure the three sides of each triangle and enter all your measurements into a table.

△	AB	BC	CA	$c°$	$a°$	$b°$	$a° + b° + c°$
(a)							
(b)							
(c)							
(d)							
(e)							

4 Which of these statements seem true from your data.

(a) $a° + b° + c°$ is about 180° for all the triangles.
(b) If AB is longer than BC then $c°$ is larger than $a°$.
(c) The longest side in the triangle is opposite the largest angle.
(d) The shortest side in the triangle is opposite the smallest angle.

B **1** Draw a circle on mm² paper, radius 4 cm (twice the diameter of the figure).

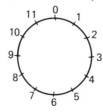

2 Mark twelve points and number them 0, 1, 2, . . . , 11.

3 Join point 0 to the point you reach after five jumps round the circle. That is 0 to 5. Now join point 5 to the point five jumps from there and so on. You should end up with a beautiful 12 pointed star.

4 Find angles which are (a) 90°, (b) 30°, (c) 120°, (d) 60° on the star.

5 Explore other patterns on another 12 point circle.

Unit P10

Exercise P24

A   Below is a plan of a kitchen drawn to the scale 1 cm = 1 m. Answer these questions carefully by measurement.

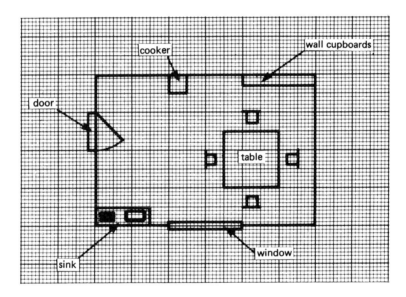

    1   How long is the kitchen?

    2   How wide is the kitchen?

    3   How wide is the window?

    4   How wide is the door?

    5   How long and wide is the table?

    6   How long and wide is the sink?

    7   How far is the cooker from the sink?

    8   How far is the draining board from the cupboards?

B   Do you think the kitchen is well arranged?

C   Measure the plan of the house below.

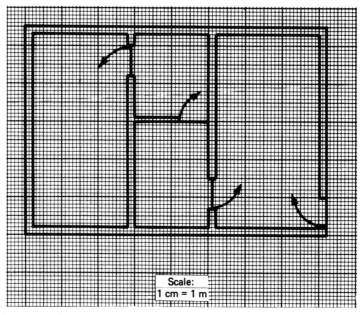

Scale:
1 cm = 1 m

(This was a design for a unit of housing by the great architect Le Corbusier. Many homes were built on the basis of this plan.)

1   What are the 'outside' measurements of the building?

2   What are the measurements of the four rooms?

3   How wide are the doorways?

4   How thick are the walls?

5   How far would you walk from the front door to the farthest corner?

6   How would you use the rooms if you and your wife/husband lived in a home designed like this?

Exercise P25

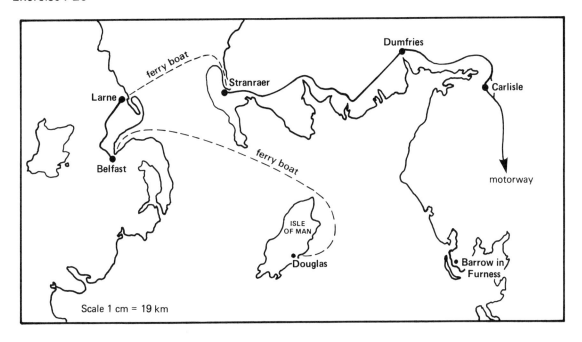

Scale 1 cm = 19 km

A This map shows an area of Great Britain which includes part of England, Scotland and also Northern Ireland. The scale is 1 cm equivalent to 14 km.

1 Measure these distances (as the crow flies.)

(a) Stranraer to Larne
(b) Stranraer to Carlisle
(c) Belfast to Douglas
(d) Douglas to Carlisle
(e) Stranraer to Barrow
(f) Dumfries to Douglas
(g) Carlisle to Belfast

2 Estimate these distances.

(a) Stranraer to Belfast by ferry boat and road
(b) Belfast to Douglas by ferry boat
(c) Dumfries to Douglas by road and ferry boat
(d) Stranraer to Barrow by coastal fishing boat

3 Discuss this comment: 'It is further from Barrow to Douglas than from Barrow to Stranraer.'

B The following plan shows part of a town. The scale is 1 cm = 100 metres.

Estimate the distances from:

1 school to the swimming pool;

2 the swimming pool to Mary's house;

3 school to the swimming pool going to the Post Office on the way;

4 school to the swimming pool to Mary's house.

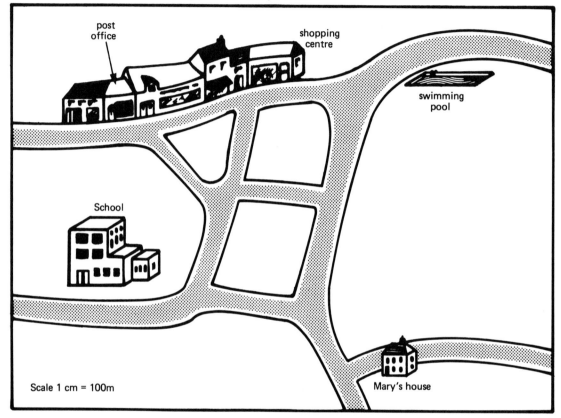

C **1** How many different ways could you go from school to the swimming pool?

2 Could you visit all four places without going back over your path?

3 How many different routes could you go from Mary's house to the Post Office?

4 Which is the shortest route from Mary's house to the Post Office?

Exercise P26

1 If a ship is travelling north, through what angle must it turn to be going:

(a) east   (b) south   (c) west?

2 A ship is travelling east and turns 90° clockwise (⟳). What is its new direction?

3 A ship is travelling south and it turns 180°. What is its new direction?

4 A ship is travelling west and it turns clockwise (⟳) to south. Through what angle has it turned?

Unit P11

Measuring rectangles

A   Measure the lengths and breadths of all the rectangles in these figures.

1

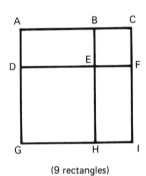

(9 rectangles)

2

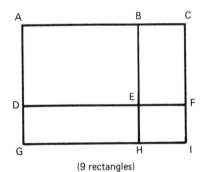

(9 rectangles)

3

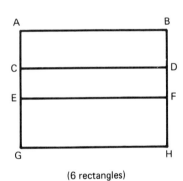

(6 rectangles)

4

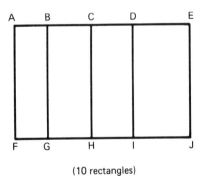

(10 rectangles)

B   Find the inside and outside perimeters of these objects.

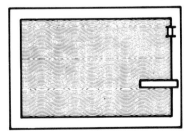

swimming pool
15m x 10m
width of edge is 1.5 metres

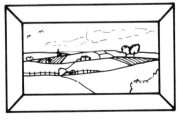

picture frame
outside dimensions: 3cm x 5cm
thickness of wood: 5mm

C **1** A field has a hedge 240 m long round it. If the field is rectangular and 80 m long, how wide is it?

2 A picture 12 cm long and 8 cm wide is put into a frame 2 cm thick all round. What are the outside measurements of the frame?

3 The pages of a book are printed with a margin 5 mm all round. The printed words form a rectangle 180 mm by 120 mm. What is the perimeter of the pages?

4 A door is being made for a rabbit hutch. It is made out of a frame 3 cm wide which is covered with wire. What is the internal perimeter of the door frame if the outside has a perimeter of 3·20 m?

Exercise P28

A Find the areas of the rectangles in these figures and add them to find the area of the whole figure.

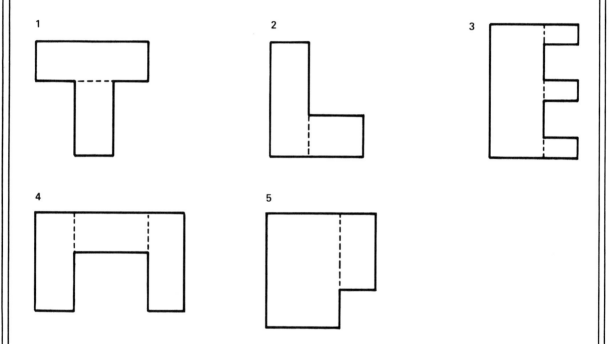

B Copy each of the figures from question **A**. Divide them into rectangles in a different way and calculate the areas using your division of the shape. Compare your results with those you obtained in question **A**.

C **1** The area of **A1** above can be found by subtracting two rectangles from a larger one leaving the T shape. Work out the areas of question **A** using subtraction of rectangles and check that it gives the same area as the method of splitting the figure into rectangles.

2 Find all the areas of question **A** using subtraction of rectangles. Check that the results agree with those you have already found.

3 Use subtraction of rectangles to find the areas of these frames (shaded).

(a)

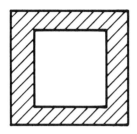

(b)

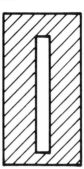

(c)

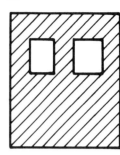

(d)

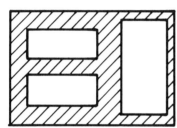

(e)

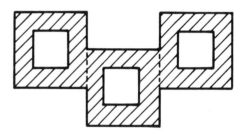

Exercise P29

A **1** Draw any circle and a pair of diameters (lines through the centre) as in the diagram.

2 Draw the figure ABCD. What sort of shape is it?

3 Repeat with another circle and another pair of diameters. What shape do you make this time? Comment.

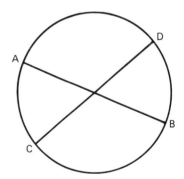

B **1** Draw any circle and divide it into two **semi-circles** with diameter XY.

2 Choose a point P on the circumference. Draw XP and YP to form the triangle XYP. What do you notice about $\hat{P}$?*

3 Repeat with a new circle and a different point P. What do you notice about XP and YP this time?

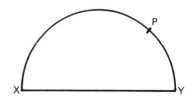

* The angle between XP and YP is called $X\hat{P}Y$ or $\hat{P}$.

Unit P12

Exercise P30

A Use a calculator to solve these problems. Where the calculator gives a long tail, take only the first two figures after the decimal point.

1 How many bolts 14 cm long can be cut from 1 m of steel?

2 How many sweaters can be made from 2 kg of wool if each sweater takes 600 g?

3 How many hours will a journey of 900 miles take at a speed of 60 miles an hour?

4 How many bags of sugar (400 g) can be made up from a 50 kg bag?

5 How many 700 ml bottles of sauce can be made from a 50 litre container?

6 If orange trees need 24 m² of land to grow properly, how many can be planted on 1 hectare of land? (1 hectare = 10 000 m²)

B Make up problems which would lead to the following divisions.

1 $100 \div 16$	**2** $1400 \div 25$	**3** $50 \div 7$
4 $200 \div 18$	**5** $1500 \div 77$	**6** $740 \div 66$

C Each of these decimals has resulted from dividing a number by less than 10. What was the number in each case? (You can tell from the 'pattern' of the decimal.)

1 $1 \div ? = 0.333\ 333\ 3$

2 $37 \div ? = 4.111\ 111\ 1$

3 $9 \div ? = 2.25$

4 $41 \div ? = 5.125$

5 $34 \div ? = 3.777\ 777\ 7$

6 $62 \div ? = 8.857\ 142\ 8$

7 $62 \div ? = 6.888\ 888\ 8$

8 $119 \div ? = 19.833\ 333$

Check on the calculator.

Tenths and hundredths

The value of a figure in a decimal can be found easily.

Example:

What is the value of the 3 in 4.735?

Find how many times you have to multiply by 10 to get the figure left of the decimal point.

$4.735 \times 10 \rightarrow 47.35$ The 3 is still on the decimal side

$4.735 \times 100 \rightarrow 473.5$ The 3 has crossed to the whole numbers

The 3 must have been 3/100 (three hundredths).

Exercise P31

A Find the values of the figures underlined.

   1 0·3<u>5</u>4   **2** 2·<u>3</u>61   **3** 4·00<u>5</u>

   4 5·0<u>8</u>6   **5** 0·000<u>7</u>   **6** 0·<u>1</u>04

B Describe the size or value that belongs to the figure underlined in these measures.

   1 £4·0<u>5</u>   **2** £5·<u>3</u>0   **3** £0·<u>6</u>   **4** £6·14<u>5</u>

   5 11·0<u>2</u> m   **6** 26·<u>5</u> cm   **7** 3·21<u>1</u> m   **8** 0·0<u>3</u> m

   9 4·60<u>5</u> km   **10** 0·3<u>6</u>5 km   **11** 4·40<u>4</u> kg   **12** 5·1<u>2</u> kg

  13 6·<u>5</u> litres   **14** 10·0<u>6</u> litres   **15** 6·<u>6</u> cl   **16** 8·<u>33</u> litres

C Which is the larger of each of these pairs of measurements?

   1 £3·2 or £3·08   **2** £4·45 or £4·70

   3 4·51 m or 4·09 m   **4** 2·33 m or 2·333 m

   5 5·647 kg or 5·670 kg   **6** 0·009 kg or 0·098 kg

   7 3·208 litres or 3·2 litres   **8** 5·00 km or 5·000 km

Exercise P32

A Write down the answers to these problems. What is the cost of the following?

   1 10 gallons of petrol at £1·80 per gallon   **2** 100 buttons at 4p each

   3 100 metres of curtain at £2·34 per metre   **4** 10 litres of oil at £1·30 per litre

   5 1000 eggs at £0·04 each   **6** 1000 bricks at £0·65 each

B Find the cost of each unit if:

   1 10 gallons of oil cost £35·40   **2** 100 metres of timber cost £175

   3 1000 litres of wine cost £1020   **4** 10 kg of rice cost £29·30

   5 100 km by taxi cost £35·50   **6** 1000 copper nails cost £2·40

C Work out the profit when a dealer:

   1 buys 100 kg of cement for £12 and sells it for 35p a kilo bag;

   2 buys 100 kg of apricots for £62·50 and sells them for 90p a kilo;

   3 buys 1000 m of timber for £140 and sells it at 30p a metre;

   4 buys 10 rings for £6·50 and sells them at £1·75 each;

   5 buys 100 lambs for £750 and sells them at £9·50 each;

   6 buys 1000 chickens for £625 and sells them at £2·30 each.

Unit P13

Exercise P33

A Multiply these in your head.

1 3×0.4 **2** 4×0.5 **3** 0.5×5 **4** 0.6×3

5 0.8×5 **6** 0.2×0.1 **7** 0.4×0.2 **8** 0.5×0.4

9 0.6×0.4 **10** 0.1×0.1

Check on the calculator, particularly the decimal point.

B **1** Complete the multiplication table which goes from 5×0.1 to 5×0.9.

$5 \times 0.1 \rightarrow 0.5$
$5 \times 0.2 \rightarrow 1.0$
$5 \times 0.3 \rightarrow 1.5$
$\vdots$
$5 \times 0.9 \rightarrow$

2 Use the table and your knowledge of the 5 times table to work out these.

(a) 5×1.6 (b) 5×2.3 (c) 5×3.5

(d) 5×2.6 (e) 5×4.2 (f) 5×5.7

3 Make similar multiplication tables for 6, 7 and 8 and use them to find the following.

(a) 6×0.3 (b) 6×1.4 (c) 6×2.7 (d) 6×5.8

(e) 7×0.4 (f) 7×2.3 (g) 7×3.5 (h) 7×4.6

(i) 8×0.6 (j) 8×2.8 (k) 8×3.4 (l) 8×5.8

Check on the calculator at the end.

C Work out these costs.

1 5 kilos of fat at £0.70 per kilo.

2 6 metres of cloth at £1.40 per metre.

3 4 km taxi ride at £1.80 per km.

4 8 m² of wood at £2.60 per m².

5 7 litres of wine at £3.50 per litre.

6 8 boxes of chocolate at £1.30 each.

7 5 bicycle tyres at £5.60 each.

8 6 shirts at £7.50 each.

Exercise P34

A The area of a rectangle is found by multiplying together its length and breadth. Find the areas of all four parts of each of these rectangles. Add the results together. Compare the total with the result of multiplying the sides of the whole rectangle. [You will need to measure.]

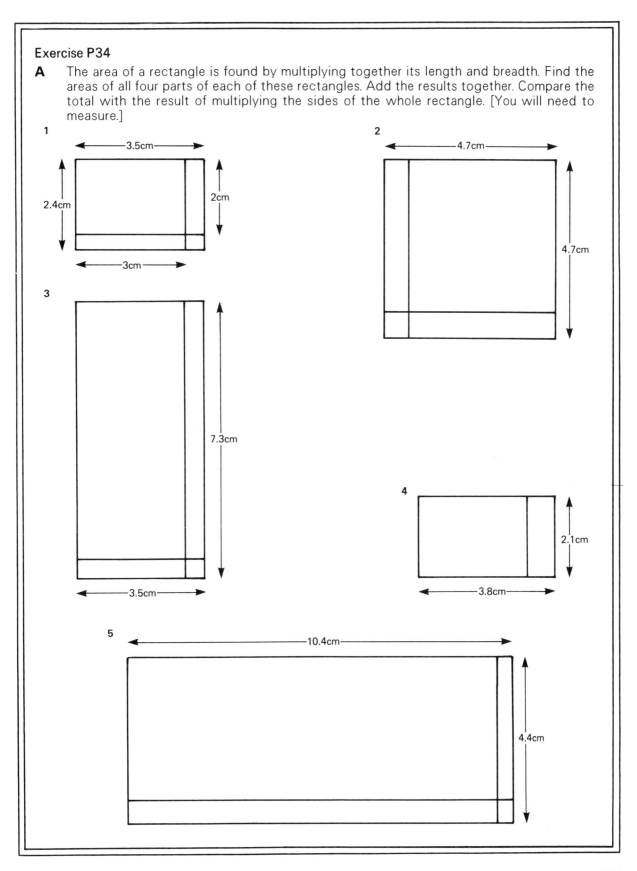

1
3.5cm
2.4cm
2cm
3cm

2
4.7cm
4.7cm

3
7.3cm
3.5cm

4
2.1cm
3.8cm

5
10.4cm
4.4cm

B Use the calculator to work out these costs and weights.

1 The cost of 1·6 kg of metal at £0·75 per kilo.

2 The cost of 3·5 kg of cheese at £1·20 per kg.

3 The cost of 650 g of syrup at £1·40 per kg.

4 The cost of 75 g of gold at £4·75 per g.

5 The weight of 2·5 m³ of stone at 2·5 tonnes per m³.*

6 The weight of 3·4 m³ of acid at 1·4 kg per litre (1 m³ = 1000 litres).

7 The weight of 4·8 m³ of iron at 7·4 tonnes per m³.

8 The weight of 3·5 m³ of sand at 1·52 tonnes per m³.

Exercise P35

Any number less than 1, when written in standard form, will have a **negative** power of 10.

Examples:

$0·4 \rightarrow 4 \times 10^{-1} = 4 \div 10$

$0·035 \rightarrow 3·5 \times 10^{-2} = 3·5 \div 100$

This tells you how many times you would have to multiply by 10 to get the number above 1.

Examples:

$0·4 \times 10 = 4·0$ (multiply by 10 once only)

$0·035 \times 10^2 = 3·5$ (multiply by 10 twice)

A Write these decimals in standard form.

1 0·3	**2** 0·7	**3** 0·08	**4** 0·04	**5** 0·06
6 0·32	**7** 0·41	**8** 0·64	**9** 0·28	**10** 0·66
11 0·002	**12** 0·023	**13** 0·608	**14** 0·055	**15** 0·567

B **1** Check each of the answers above by multiplying the 10s in the standard form by the original decimal. You should get a number between 1 and 9·99.

2 Write these in decimal form.

(a) 2×10^{-1} (b) $4·6 \times 10^{-1}$ (c) $5·5 \times 10^{-2}$

(d) $5·8 \times 10^{-3}$ (e) $6·07 \times 10^{-2}$ (f) $3·3 \times 10^{-2}$

(g) $5·81 \times 10^{-3}$ (h) $6·59 \times 10^{-6}$

C Write these facts using decimal form instead of standard form for the numbers.

1 Light travels one mile in $5·376 \times 10^{-6}$ seconds.

2 A hydrogen atom weighs $1·67 \times 10^{-27}$ kg.

3 Sound travels 1 metre in 3×10^{-3} seconds.

4 A molecule of protein weighs $2·5 \times 10^{-19}$ g.

5 A typical germ weighs 8×10^{-7} g.

*Note: Since   1 tonne = 1000 kg   } a substance will have the same weight in tonnes per m³ as it has in kg
           1 m³   = 1000 litres } per litre.

Unit P14

Subtraction of fractions

There are three ways of subtracting fractions and these are the same for addition.

Method 1

Subtract the values

$$1/2 - \quad 1/3 \qquad = 0{\cdot}166\ 66$$

$$0{\cdot}5 - \quad 0{\cdot}333\ 33$$

Method 2

Find equivalent fractions which have the same divisor (second number)

$$1/2 - \quad 1/3 = 1/6$$

$$3/6 - \quad 2/6$$

Method 3

Use the keyboard sequence for $a/b - c/d$ which is

| d | × | a | ÷ | b | − | c | ÷ | d | = |

Example:

$1/2 - 1/3$

| 3 | × | 1 | ÷ | 2 | − | 1 | ÷ | 3 | = |

Display   3   3   1   3   2   1·5   1   0·5   3   0·166 66

NOTE: Method 2 gives the result as a fraction.
Methods 1 and 3 give the result as a decimal which is the value of the fraction.

Exercise P36

A Use method 2 to subtract these fractions. Check by one of the other methods on your calculator.

1 $1/2 - 1/4$	**2** $3/4 - 1/8$	**3** $1/5 - 1/10$	**4** $1/2 - 1/8$
5 $3/4 - 1/4$	**6** $1/2 - 1/12$	**7** $3/4 - 3/12$	**8** $1/2 - 1/5$

B Use method 1 to subtract these fractions.

1 1/4 − 1/5   **2** 1/3 − 1/8   **3** 1/4 − 1/16   **4** 2/3 − 1/2

5 4/7 − 1/2   **6** 3/8 − 4/19   **7** 5/80 − 3/100   **8** 4/10 − 3/17

C Use method 3 to subtract these fractions. Then use method 2 to find the result as a fraction. Check that the value of the fraction is the same as the answer you obtained by method 3.

1 3/4 − 1/2   **2** 5/8 − 3/16   **3** 7/9 − 2/3

4 5/8 − 1/12   **5** 3/10 − 1/5   **6** 3/10 − 3/100

7 14/100 − 1/10   **8** 3/4 − 13/100

Multiplication of fractions

1 When two fractions have to be multiplied the figures are entered straight into the calculator.

Example:

2/3 × 4/5

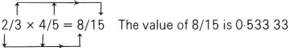

Display   *0*   *2*   *2*   *3*   *0·66*   *4*   *2·66*   *5*   *0·533 33*

2 The result can be obtained as a fraction by forming a fraction whose first number is the product of the first numbers and whose second number is the product of the second numbers.

Example:

2/3 × 4/5 = 8/15   The value of 8/15 is 0·533 33

Exercise P37

A Find the results of these multiplications by both methods and compare results.

1 1/2 × 3/4   **2** 3/4 × 5/6   **3** 2/3 × 3/10   **4** 5/8 × 4/12

5 3/7 × 2/9   **6** 2/5 × 3/10   **7** 3/5 × 7/11   **8** 3/10 × 2/3

B Show that you could get the same result by finding the values first and then multiplying.

C Find the areas of these rectangles.

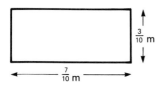

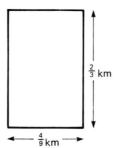

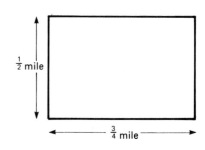

$\updownarrow \frac{3}{8}$ inch

←————— 11¼ inches —————→

D Work out these in your head. (Remember × can be replaced by 'of'.)

1 1/2 × 14   **2** 1/2 × 7   **3** 1/4 × 6   **4** 1/4 × 10

5 1/2 × 1/3   **6** 1/2 × 1/4   **7** 1/2 × 1/10   **8** 1/4 × 3/4

Division of fractions

The safest way of dividing one fraction by another is to divide the values.

Example:

3/5 ÷ 1/4 = 2·4   This gives a decimal result.

0·6 ÷ 0·25

Note: The result is much larger than the fraction you started with.

Exercise P38

A Divide these fractions.

1 1/2 ÷ 1/4   **2** 3/8 ÷ 3/4   **3** 7/10 ÷ 3/4   **4** 5/6 ÷ 2/6

5 7/9 ÷ 1/7   **6** 10/12 ÷ 3/4   **7** 2/1* ÷ 1/2   **8** 3/1 ÷ 2/5

9 5/1 ÷ 1/10   **10** 7 ÷ 1/2   **11** 9 ÷ 1/3   **12** 15 ÷ 1/4

B The work on the calculator can be done simply if the following sequence is followed:

$a/b \div c/d$:   [c] [d] [×] [a] [÷] [b] [÷] [c] [=]

Run through the previous exercise using this sequence and check that you get the same result.

The effect of multiplying by d to start with is to change the calculation to division by a whole number. For example, 2 ÷ 3/4 becomes 8 ÷ 3 which is an **equivalent** division.

C The question 7 ÷ 1/2 gives the result 14 which suggests that dividing by 1/2 is the same as multiplying by 2.

Check with the calculator that these pairs give the same result.

1 1/2 ÷ 1/4 and 1/2 × 4/1   **2** 3 ÷ 2/5 and 3 × 5/2

3 4 ÷ 2/3 and 4 × 3/2   **4** 7 ÷ 3/10 and 7 × 10/3

5 3/4 ÷ 5/8 and 3/4 × 8/5   **6** 5/7 ÷ 3/16 and 5/7 × 16/3

*2/1 is the same as 2.

Unit P 15

Exercise P39

A

1 Cut four strips of card all the same length. In each strip make a hole at each end the same distance from the end of the strip each time. Join the strips with four treasury pins so that each pin joins two strips. Describe the shape you have made. Move the strips around on a table opening the angles. Make drawings to show what happens to the shape as you change the angles.

2 List some measurements of the shape which do not change however you arrange it.

3 List some properties of the shape which do not change however you arrange it; in particular, properties of the diagonals.

4 List some things which do change as your shape is moved about.

B You will need some scrap paper and a pair of scissors.

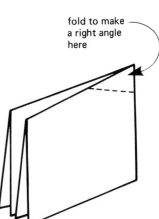

fold to make a right angle here

1 Fold a piece of paper and make a right angle (shown in the diagram). Draw a straight line across the right angle and cut along the line you have drawn. What will be the shape of the piece of paper you have cut off?

2 Make different shapes of the same sort by cutting along different lines. Start with a new right angle fold each time.

3 What do the pieces you have cut off tell you about:

   (a) the diagonals of a rhombus?
   (b) the opposite angles of a rhombus?
   (c) the axes of symmetry of a rhombus?

C Make a 36 dot square grid on graph paper by putting dots where 1 cm lines meet.

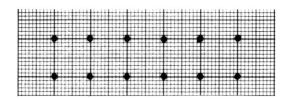

1 Draw as many different rhombuses as you can with all four corners on grid points. Measure the diagonals, angles and side lengths for each rhombus. Enter your results in a table.

2 Look at the rhombuses below.

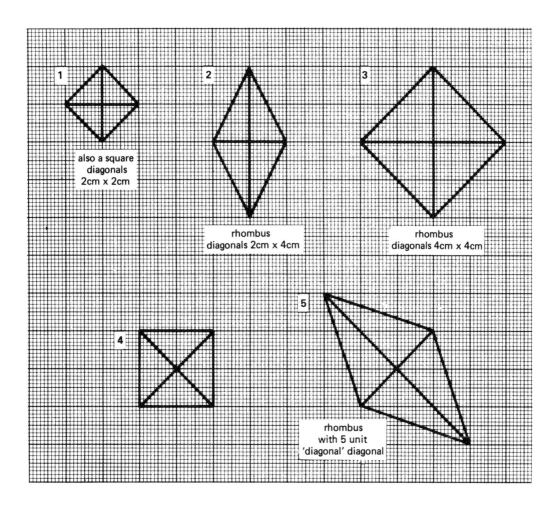

1 also a square
diagonals
2cm x 2cm

2 rhombus
diagonals 2cm x 4cm

3 rhombus
diagonals 4cm x 4cm

4

5 rhombus
with 5 unit
'diagonal' diagonal

There are two sorts shown, those with vertical and horizontal diagonals and those with 'diagonal' diagonals.

(a) How many different rhombuses can you draw with a 6 cm diagonal?
(b) How many different rhombuses can you draw with a 6 unit 'diagonal' diagonal?
(c) Can you find any rhombuses (or tilted squares) that are different from both the sorts shown in the diagram.

Exercise P40

Isosceles triangles have been used for thousands of years in making patterns. Look at the examples and then design some patterns of your own on mm² paper.

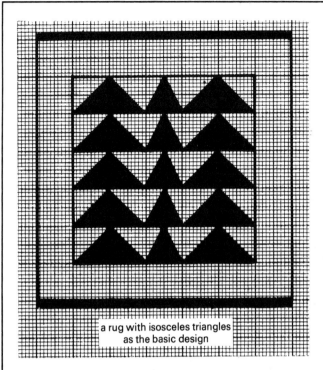

a rug with isosceles triangles as the basic design

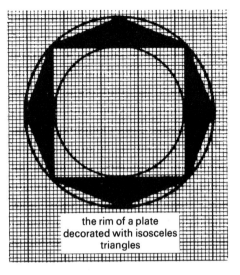

the rim of a plate decorated with isosceles triangles

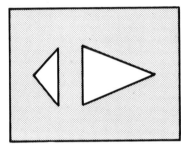

Template for two related isosceles triangles

You may find it easier to cut out isosceles triangles from a piece of card to make a 'template'. You can then make as many repeats of the triangles as you like by drawing inside the template.

Angles in an isosceles triangle

Since the angles of an isosceles triangle add up to 180°, it is possible to find all the angles if you know one of them.

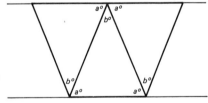

Exercise P41

A   Explain why the above diagram shows that the sum of all three angles in an isosceles triangle must be 180°.

B   Find the other two angles of an isosceles triangle if the angle between the equal sides is:

1 40°   **2** 60°   **3** 18°   **4** 80°   **5** 100°   **6** 120°

C   Find the other two angles of an isosceles triangle if one of the equal angles is:

1 25°   **2** 36°   **3** 60°   **4** 70°   **5** 45°   **6** 75°

Unit P16

Exercise P42

A Parallel lines are to be found in many patterns.

1 Write down all the parallel lines you can find in the **translation** of the letter E below.

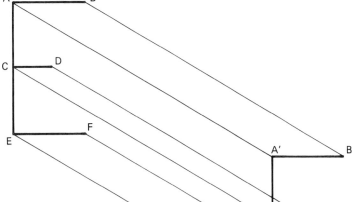

2 Write down all the parallel lines you can see in the following figures.

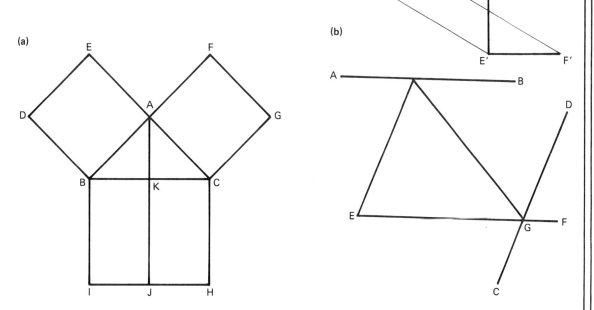

(a)

(b)

B These figures are drawn on **isometric** paper. This paper is ruled with three sets of parallel lines.

    The lines of one set make an angle of 60° with the lines of another set. This grid made up of three sets of parallel lines all at 60°, is called an isometric grid.

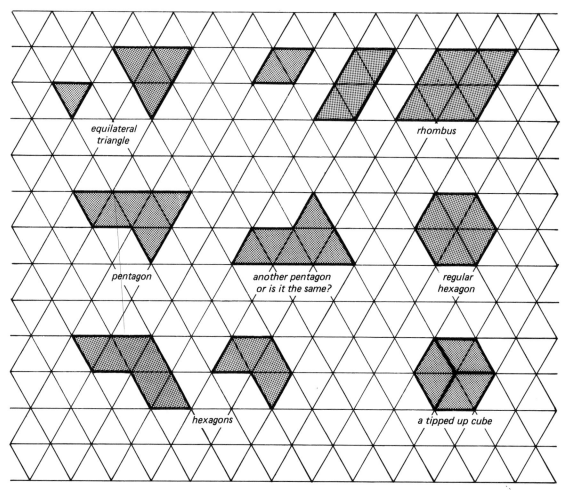

1 Obtain (or draw) some isometric paper and draw the following shapes on it.

  (a) Four different sizes of equilateral triangle
  (b) Four different sizes of rhombus
  (c) Four different sizes of regular hexagon

2 Draw as many different kinds of pentagon as you can.

3 Draw as many different shapes as you can that enclose:

  (a) 4 triangles   (b) 5 triangles   (c) 6 triangles

4 Draw these shapes.

  (a) A parallelogram that encloses 6 triangles
  (b) A triangle that encloses 9 triangles
  (c) A quadrilateral that encloses 5 triangles

C 1 Draw three parallel lines equal distances apart. Think carefully about how you can do this. Draw a line across them.

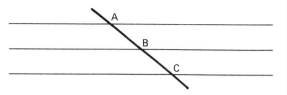

2 Measure the distances AB and BC. What do you notice?

3 Draw another line across the three parallels and mark the points of intersection D, E, F. Measure DE and EF.

4 What would you expect if you drew another line XYZ across the parallel lines?

5 Do you agree with this statement? 'A set of parallel lines which cuts one line into equal parts will do the same for any other line.'

Exercise P43

A Find the value of the angles marked $x°$ and $y°$ in each of these figures.

1

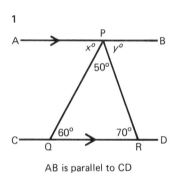

AB is parallel to CD

2

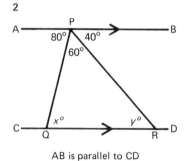

AB is parallel to CD

3

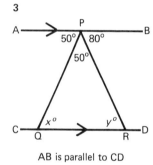

AB is parallel to CD

B 1 Add up the three angles inside the triangles in **1–3** above. Check they come to 180° each time.

2 Find $x°$ and $y°$ in each of the figures below.

(a)

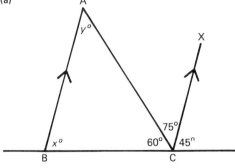

AB is parallel to CX

(b)

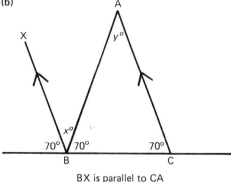

BX is parallel to CA

3 Add up the angles inside the triangles. Do they also add up to 180°?

Exercise P44

Sets of parallel lines are used to form grids in maps.

A **1** This map uses letters and numbers to name the spaces on the grid. This helps to find streets and places if you do not know the area.

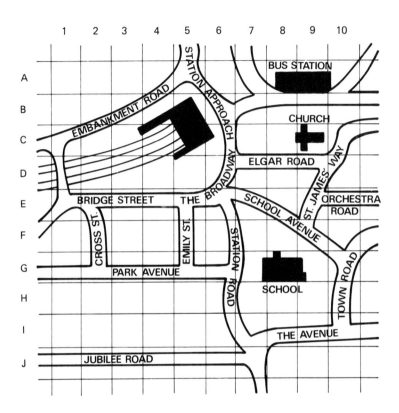

Find these street junctions.

(a) School Avenue and Town Road (G, 10)
(b) Cross St and Bridge St (E, 2)
(c) St James' Way and Orchestra Rd
(d) Jubilee Road and Station Road
(e) Emily St and The Broadway

2 The space name is called a **map reference**. What are the map references for the following?

(a) The school
(b) St James' Church
(c) The bus station
(d) The junction of Town Road and The Avenue
(e) The junction of Cross St and Park Avenue

Unit P 17

Exercise P45

A   Find a suitable object to include in these sets.

    1 {fork, spade, pick, . . .}

    2 {Jenny, Mary, Liz, Brenda, . . .}

    3 {1/2, 1/4, 1/8, 1/3, . . .}

    4 {pigeon, sparrow, hawk, . . .}

    5 {daisy, tulip, daffodil, . . .}

    6 {Ford, BL, Fiat, VW, . . .}

    7 {sweet, sour, salty, . . .}

    8 {cat, dog, rabbit, . . .}

B   The sets A, B, C, D are:

A = {George, Henry, William, . . .}

B = {spanner, pliers, hammer, . . .}

C = {marrow, cabbage, sprouts, . . .}

D = {coffee, tea, cola, . . .}

    1 Write down two more members of each set.

    2 Which of these statements are true and which are not true (false). Remember $\in$ means 'belongs to'.

        (a) saw $\in B$ (b) carrots $\in D$ (c) beer $\in C$

        (d) chisel $\in A$ (e) James $\in A$ (f) lettuce $\in C$

        (g) milk $\in D$ (h) plane $\in C$

    3 Which of these statements are true and which are false. Remember $\notin$ means 'does not belong to'.

        (a) screwdriver $\notin B$ (b) Richard $\notin B$ (c) sausage $\notin C$

        (d) lemonade $\notin D$ (e) cauliflower $\notin C$ (f) John $\notin A$

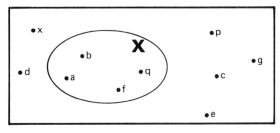

C X is the set of points inside the boundary. Which of these are true?

    1 $p \in X$ **2** $q \in X$ **3** $d \in X$ **4** $f \in X$ **5** $b \notin X$

    6 $e \notin X$ **7** $x \notin X$ **8** $a \notin X$

Exercise P46

A Find four more members of each of these sets.

    1 $\{6, 12, 16, 22, \ldots\}$ **2** $\{3, 7, 11, 15, \ldots\}$

    3 $\{1, 2, 6, 24, \ldots\}$ **4** $\{1, 1{\cdot}5, 2{\cdot}0, 2{\cdot}5, \ldots\}$

    5 $\{275, 250, 225, 200, \ldots\}$ **6** $\{2, 22, 222, \ldots\}$

B $A = \{1, 3, 5, 7, \ldots\}$ $S = \{1, 4, 9, 16, \ldots\}$
     $T = \{3, 6, 9, 12, \ldots\}$ $P = \{2, 3, 5, 7, 11, \ldots\}$

    1 Find another way of describing the members of the four sets A, T, S and P.

    2 Which of these statements are true and which are false?

        (a) $47 \in A$ (b) $15 \in S$ (c) $49 \in A$ (d) $49 \in S$
        (e) $47 \in P$ (f) $15 \in T$ (g) $49 \in P$ (h) $143 \in P$

    3 Which of these statements are true and which are false?

        (a) $25 \notin A$ (b) $11 \notin P$ (c) $54 \notin T$ (d) $81 \notin P$
        (e) $100 \notin P$ (f) $25 \notin S$ (g) $44 \notin A$ (h) $81 \notin S$

C **1** In each of the figures a set of shapes can be found. Copy the figure and draw in two more shapes of the same set.

(a)

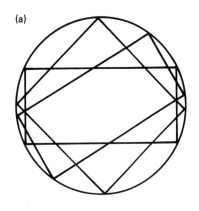

(b)

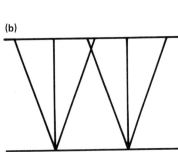

(c)

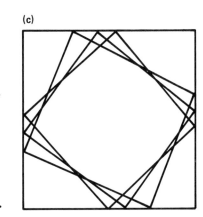

2 In each of the diagrams below one line does not belong to the set. Pick it out and explain how it is different from the others.

(a)

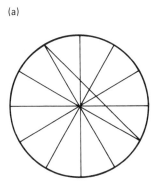

(b)

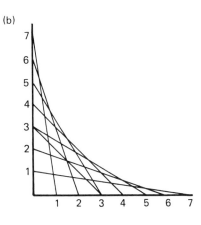

(c)

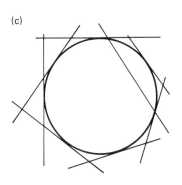

(d)

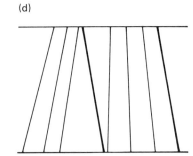

Unit P18

Exercise P47

A   A code is made by mapping {A, B, C, D, ..., Z} on to {1, 2, 3, 4, ..., 26} but moving the code round four places so that W→ 1, X→ 2, Y→ 3, Z→ 4, A→ 5, B→ 6 and so on.

1   Write these words in code.

   (a) ATTACK   (b) KING   (c) QUEEN

2   Decode these.

   (a) 232422516922223   (b) 8191824/10192211924
   (c) 23122524/2520   (d) 813181892223/229583

3   Another way to use this code would be to map the letters to letters four on and then use A→ 1, B→ 2, C→ 3, etc, to put the code into numbers.

   Try this for the words attack, king and queen. Do you get the same result as in question **1**?

B   A code may be constructed using a grid.*

5	A	I	J	N	O
4	V	B	H	K	M
3	S	W	C	G	L
2	Q	T	X	D	F
1	P	R	U	Y	E
	1	2	3	4	5

The letters may be placed in the grid in any order, but the person receiving the message will need a copy of the grid before he can decode. Z is kept as the letter Z if needed.

Each letter is given an address by a pair of numbers.

e.g. A→ (15), B→ (24) and so on.

(The first number shows the box number along from the left while the second number shows the box number up from the bottom.)

1   Put this message into grid code: PLEASE TELEPHONE

2   Decode these messages.

   (a) 341511114124252122344421541
   (b) 44515111222141254543

* Grid code is very difficult to break because there are 15 billion billion different possible arrangements for the letters in the grid!

C   Make up some code system of your own and send some messages to a friend. You could add some 'dummy numbers' to make the code more difficult. These are numbers that have no letter attached to them. They just confuse other people who look for a letter when there is none.

Exercise P48

In a code we can map each letter on to another one. A→B, B→C and so on. We call this mapping the alphabet on to itself.

When we change numbers (by adding on 5 for example) we call this mapping the set of natural numbers on to itself.

A   **1**   What set of numbers do you get from mapping the natural numbers in the following ways?

(a) $n \rightarrow n + 2$ (c) $n \rightarrow 2n$ (this means $n + n$)
(b) $n \rightarrow n + 5$ (d) $n \rightarrow 3n$

2   What mapping would produce these changes?

(a) $1 \rightarrow 5$ (b) $1 \rightarrow 2$ (c) $1 \rightarrow 0$
 $2 \rightarrow 6$ $2 \rightarrow 4$ $2 \rightarrow 1$
 $3 \rightarrow 7$ $3 \rightarrow 6$ $3 \rightarrow 2$
 $4 \rightarrow 8$ $4 \rightarrow 8$ $4 \rightarrow 3$

3   Change each of these sets by the mapping shown.

(a) {2, 3, 6, 8} by $n \rightarrow n - 2$ (b) {3, 5, 10, 15} by $n \rightarrow 2n$
(c) {4, 8, 16, 32} by $n \rightarrow \frac{1}{2}n$ (d) {5, 10, 15, 20} by $n \rightarrow n \times 0.2$
(e) {2, 3, 6, 10} by $n \rightarrow 2n + 3$ (f) {2, 4, 5, 10} by $n \rightarrow 2n - 1$

B   Sometimes you will want to know the number you started with in a mapping.

Example: mapping $n \rightarrow n + 3$ $? \rightarrow 10$

You can see that 7 would map on to 10 under this mapping.

1   Find the numbers to replace x in these mappings.

(a) $n \rightarrow 2n$ (i) $x \rightarrow 10$ (ii) $x \rightarrow 30$ (iii) $x \rightarrow 15$
                                  (iv) $x \rightarrow 20$ (v) $x \rightarrow 24$ (vi) $x \rightarrow 0$

(b) $n \rightarrow n + 5$ (i) $x \rightarrow 10$ (ii) $x \rightarrow 19$ (iii) $x \rightarrow 0$
                                  (iv) $x \rightarrow 35$ (v) $x \rightarrow 5$ (vi) $x \rightarrow 2$

(c) $n \rightarrow n - 3$ (i) $x \rightarrow 10$ (ii) $x \rightarrow 12$ (iii) $x \rightarrow 0$
                                  (iv) $x \rightarrow 18$ (v) $x \rightarrow 3$ (vi) $x \rightarrow -2$

(d) $n \rightarrow 2n + 2$ (i) $x \rightarrow 10$ (ii) $x \rightarrow 30$ (iii) $x \rightarrow 0$
                                  (iv) $x \rightarrow 14$ (v) $x \rightarrow 5$ (vi) $x \rightarrow 2$

2   Find the mapping first and then find the numbers to replace x.

(a) $1 \rightarrow 3$ (b) $1 \rightarrow 4$ (c) $1 \rightarrow 2$
       $2 \rightarrow 6$ $2 \rightarrow 6$ $2 \rightarrow 5$
       $3 \rightarrow 9$ $3 \rightarrow 8$ $3 \rightarrow 8$
       $4 \rightarrow 12$ $4 \rightarrow 10$ $4 \rightarrow 11$
(i) $x \rightarrow 15$ (i) $x \rightarrow 22$ (i) $7 \rightarrow x$
(ii) $x \rightarrow 21$ (ii) $x \rightarrow 34$ (ii) $9 \rightarrow x$
(iii) $10 \rightarrow x$ (iii) $41 \rightarrow x$ (iii) $10 \rightarrow x$

Unit P20

Exercise P49
Symmetry and biscuit tins

You can study the symmetry of a shape by thinking of it as a lid on a biscuit tin.

A   Cut out, from squared paper, lids which would fit exactly on to the 'tins' drawn below. Mark the lids to match the corners. Start off with A/A, B/B, C/C, D/D. This means that corner A of the lid is over corner A of the box, etc.

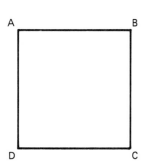  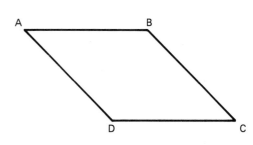

    1   Write down all the different ways the first lid will fit the box, without the lid being turned over. Do the same for the other two shapes (rectangle and parallelogram).

    2   Now write down the ways the lid will fit if the lid is turned over. Do the same for the other two shapes.

B **1**   Repeat the study for **A** with these shapes.

(a) Hexagon    **(b)** Rhombus

(c) Circle   **(d)** Trapezium

Exercise P50

Symmetry in nature and design

Nature makes use of symmetry in plants and animals. For example, we need two eyes to fix distances, one is not enough.

A Look at the drawings of insects. Which parts are symmetrical? Why do you think the insects have grown in this symmetrical form?

Can you find any parts of the insect which are not symmetrical?

B These drawings of bridges and aircraft show symmetry. Why do you think symmetry is necessary? What do you think would happen to an unsymmetrical aircraft or an unsymmetrical bridge?

swept back wing

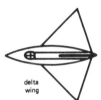

delta wing

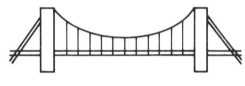

C Copy these designs on to mm² paper. Pick out the basic shape. Does the basic shape have an axis of symmetry or a centre of symmetry?

Use the ideas to make some designs of your own.

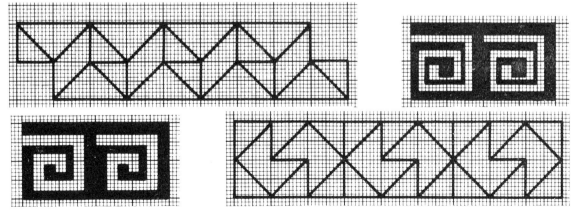

Unit P21

Exercise P51

A   **1**   Write down the co-ordinates of the points marked with letters.

      2   What do you notice about the coordinates of

        (a) B, G and E?
        (b) F, G and C?
        (c) A, G and D?

        How do the co-ordinates show in numbers the special position of G in the drawing?

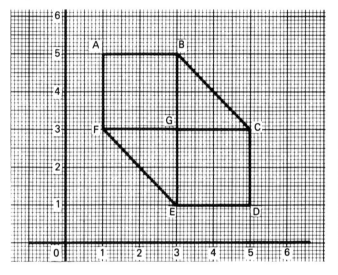

      3   Write down the co-ordinates of the points of the stars in the following figures.

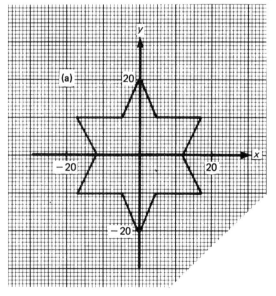

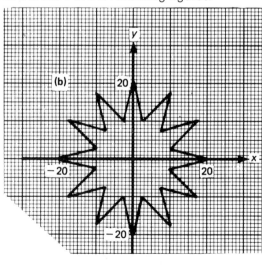

180

What do you notice when you add:

(a) co-ordinates of opposite points together?

(b) co-ordinates of points which are reflections in the x axis?

(c) co-ordinates of points which are reflections in the y axis?

Copy the stars on to mm² paper and colour them.

B Draw pairs of axes on graph paper and mark six members of each of these sets of points.

1 Points which are 12 mm from the x axis.

2 Points which are 9 mm from the y axis.

3 Points which are the same distance from the x axis and the y axis.

4 Points whose distance from the x axis is 5 mm more than their distance from the y axis.

5 Points whose distance from the x axis is 3 mm less than their distance from the y axis.

6 Points whose distance from the x axis is twice their distance from the y axis.

C Mark these sets of points on graph paper. What shape is made when you join the points up?

1 (1, 1), (2, 1), (1, 2), (2, 2)　　　　　**2** (0, 0), (2, 2), (4, 4), (6, 6)

3 (1, 1), (3, 1), (4, 2), (2, 2)　　　　　**4** (1, 1), (2, 2), (3, 3), (4, 4)

5 (1, 2), (2, 4), (3, 6)　　　　　　　　**6** (4, 2), (4, 4), (4, 5), (4, 6)

7 (2, 3), (4, 3), (5, 3), (7, 3)　　　　　**8** (0, 3), (1, 5), (2, 7), (3, 9)

Exercise P52

Graphs of functions

A **1** Write down the image set of the numbers $(-5, -4, -3, -2, -1, 0, 1, 2, 3, 4, 5)$ under these mappings.

(a) $x \rightarrow x + 1$　　　　　(b) $x \rightarrow x + 4$　　　　　(c) $x \rightarrow 2x$
(d) $x \rightarrow x - 2$　　　　　(e) $x \rightarrow x - 6$　　　　　(f) $x \rightarrow 2x - 1$

2 Write down the ordered pairs which arise from these mappings, from $x = -5$ to $x = 5$.

(a) $x \rightarrow x + 4$　　　　　　　　(b) $x \rightarrow 2x - 1$

3 Use the ordered pairs of **2** to draw graphs of the following from $x = -5$ to $x = 5$.

(a) $y = x + 4$　　　　　　　　(b) $y = 2x - 1$

B **1** Draw a careful graph of the function $y = 2x + 1$ from $x = 0$ to $x = 6$.

First make a complete table of the mappings in this form.

x	0	1	2	3	4	5	6
y	1	3					

2 Use your graph to find the value of y when x is:
(a) 2·5　　　(b) 3·5　　　(c) 4·2　　　(d) 4·7

Check by calculating the result of mapping 2·5 etc. under $x \rightarrow 2x + 1$.

3 Draw, on the same axes, the graphs of these functions, from $x = 0$ to $x = 6$.

(a) $y = 2x + 1$　　(b) $y = 2x + 3$　　(c) $y = 2x + 5$　　(d) $y = 2x - 1$

What do you notice about the four graphs?

Unit P22

A **1** Write each of these percentages in fraction and decimal form.

(a) 50%   (b) 25%   (c) 30%   (d) 45%   (e) 65%
(f) 75%   (g) 100%   (h) 120%   (i) 125%   (j) 10%
(k) 42%   (l) 36%   (m) 28%   (n) 77%

2 Write these fractions as percentages. Convert them to decimals first.

(a) 3/5   (b) 5/10   (c) 25/40   (d) 15/30
(e) 16/25   (f) 3/8   (g) 4/9   (h) 5/12

3 Write these decimals as percentages.

(a) 0·4   (b) 0·7   (c) 0·65   (d) 0·88
(e) 0·97   (f) 1·05   (g) 1·20   (h) 0·6666

4 Write these marks as percentage marks. Convert to decimals first.

(a) 7 out of 10   (b) 5 out of 10   (c) 6 out of 20
(d) 12 out of 20   (e) 15 out of 20   (f) 19 out of 25
(g) 22 out of 25   (h) 25 out of 40

B **1** Work out the following.

(a) 8% of £10   (b) 15% of £1·60   (c) 10% of £2·30
(d) 22% of £4·80   (e) 5% of £16   (f) 15% of £4·80
(g) 25% of £16   (h) 30% of £7·50   (i) 24% of £5·40
(j) 36% of £50   (k) 75% of £80   (l) 77% of £91·50

2 Estimate these without using the calculator. Indicate how you work it out.

(a) 10% of 2 km   (b) 10% of 8 metres   (c) 10% of 5 kg
(d) 10% of 6 litres (e) 20% of 12 metres (f) 20% of 3 km
(g) 20% of 9 kg   (h) 50% of 6 km   (i) 20% of 10 litres
(j) 50% of 18 metres (k) 50% of 14 kg   (l) 50% of 22 litres

3 Work out these with the calculator. Write your answer as a sentence each time.

(a) 10% of 4850 people voted Conservative. How many people was this?
(b) 22% of 5250 cars had worn tyres. How many cars was this?
(c) 36% of 7825 people disliked noise. How many people was this?
(d) 28% of the 630 acre farm was grass. How many acres of grass?
(e) 37% of the 2560 apple trees gave eating apples. How many trees were not eating apples trees?

C **1** Write these statements in percentage form.

    (a) 7 out of 100 new cars give some trouble in the first month.
    (b) 6 people out of 200 read the Daily Blaze.
    (c) 1 person in 25 eats too much.
    (d) Only 4 people out of 10 take enough exercise.

2 In two tests the teacher marked one out of 70 and the other out of 80. What percentage would these marks be?

    (a) 35 out of 70   (b) 40 out of 70   (c) 7 out of 70
    (d) 15 out of 70   (e) 42 out of 70   (f) 50 out of 70

3 In another test, out of 40, the marks were 6, 9, 14, 14, 17, 17, 18, 19, 23, 24, 24, 26, 27, 29, 30, 31, 31, 33, 35, 35, 36, 37, 39.

    (a) How many children scored more than 90%?
    (b) How many children scored more than 70%?
    (c) How many children scored more than 50%?
    (d) How many children scored under 40%?
    (e) How many children scored under 20%?

Exercise P54

Comparing by percentage

A **1** In class 2A, 27 out of 31 children could swim and in class 2B, 25 out of 28 could swim. Which class had the higher percentage of swimmers?

2 Mary got 37 right out of 50 in an English test and 40 right out of 60 in a Science test. In which test did she do better?

3 60 boys and 80 girls were asked if they would like to learn to ride horses. 45 of the girls said yes but only 25 of the boys wanted to learn. Would you say that riding horses is twice as popular with girls as with boys?

4 The same children were asked if they would like to learn to drive at school. This time 54 of the boys and 61 of the girls said yes. Find the percentage of boys and girls who wanted to learn to drive?

Increasing and decreasing

B When prices go up by 10%, the new price is found by adding 10% to the old price.

Example:

A train fare   £7·50
       10%   £0·75
  new price   £8·25

1 Find the new prices when these go up by 10%.

    (a) Petrol, £1·20 a gallon   (b) 5 litres of paint, £6·90
    (c) A teapot, £4·50   (d) A coat, £24
    (e) Leg of lamb, £1·80 per lb   (f) A bike, £76

2 Find the new prices when these go up by 20%.

    (a) A car, £2400   (b) A tennis racquet, £16
    (c) A holiday in Spain, £160   (d) An air ticket to Australia, £600

3 Find the new price when these go down by 10%.

    (a) A motor bike, £1800   (b) A rucksack, £16
    (c) A coffee pot, £4·80   (d) A gas cooker, £176
    (e) A tent, £96   (f) A fishing rod, £14·50

Unit P23

Exercise P55

A Find the first number that was put into the calculator (n).

		Display			Display
1	$n + 3 =$	17	**2**	$n - 5 =$	12
3	$n - 12 =$	12	**4**	$n + 16 =$	48
5	$n + 50 =$	202	**6**	$n - 47 =$	71
7	$n + 100 =$	105	**8**	$n - 135 =$	4
9	$n + 462 =$	666	**10**	$n - 852 =$	27
11	$n + 523 =$	718	**12**	$n - 714 =$	235

Check by running n through the programme each time.

B Find the first number that was put into the calculator (f).

		Display			Display
1	$f \times 3 =$	264	**2**	$f \times 5 =$	1070
3	$f \times 10 =$	670	**4**	$f \times 14 =$	98
5	$f \times 52 =$	1196	**6**	$f \times 72 =$	2952
7	$f \div 6 =$	3	**8**	$f \div 9 =$	10
9	$f \div 17 =$	15	**10**	$f \div 27 =$	12
11	$f \div 39 =$	22	**12**	$f \div 66 =$	19

C Find the number that was put into the calculator.

		Display			Display
1	$n + 3 \cdot 5 =$	11	**2**	$n - 1 \cdot 6 =$	4.2
3	$f \times 3 \cdot 6 =$	4.8	**4**	$f \div 2 \cdot 4 =$	7
5	$n \times 3 + 5 =$	23	**6**	$n + 4 \times 7 =$	28
7	$n - 5 \times 36 =$	36	**8**	$n + 3 \div 4 =$	1.8
9	$n \div 4 + 3 =$	4.25	**10**	$n + 5 \div 3 =$	0.4
11	$f \times 4 \div 3 =$	36	**12**	$f \div 6 \cdot 4 \times 1 \cdot 3 =$	4.468 75

Exercise P56

A Find the value of the letter in each of these equations. Use your calculator where necessary.

1 $x + 7 = 9$	**2** $y - 3 = 5$	**3** $q + 8 = 17$
4 $a \times 3 = 27$	**5** $b \div 5 = 4$	**6** $c \times 12 = 48$
7 $d \div 20 = 45$	**8** $3 \times f = 45$	**9** $4 \div f = 6$

B   Use your calculator to solve these equations (find the value of the letter).

1   $x + 3.5 = 12.7$ 2 $x - 4.6 = 4.6$ 3 $y + 1.02 = 2.3$

4   $y - 3.8 = 0$ 5 $p \times 4.2 = 7$ 6 $q \times 1.6 = 2.6$

7   $r \times 3 = 11.4$ 8 $s \times 1.02 = 6$ 9 $a \div 5 = 3.1$

10   $b \div 2.4 = 30$ 11 $c \div 1.4 = 4.1$ 12 $d \div 0.3 = 3$

Check each time that you have found the correct value by inserting the number in the equation.

C   Which of the values given make the equation true (are solutions to the equation*)?

1   $x - 3.4 = 7$, values 3.4, 7, 3.6, 10.4

2   $x - 4.05 = 6.20$, values 4.05, 6.20, 10.25, 1.15

3   $17 - y = 6$, values 11, 23, 6, 17

4   $14.5 - y = 3.95$, values 3.95, 28.45, 10.55

5   $p \times 3.6 = 4.2$, values 1, 3.6, 4.2, 7.8, 1.166\dot{6}

6   $1.4 \times p = 11.2$, values 5, 12.6, 9.8, 6, 8

7   $x \div 3 = 9$, values 3, 9, 0.333 3, 27

8   $8 \div x = 4.72$, values 0.509, 1, 1.694 9, 4.5

Exercise P57

A   Write these in short form.

1   $x + x + x + x + x + x + x + x + x$

2   $a + a + a + a + a$

3   $y \times y$

4   $p \times p \times p \times p$

5   $q \times q \times q \times q \times q \times q \times q \times q$

6   $(y \times y \times y) + (y \times y \times y)$

B   Write these out in long form.

1   x^3 2 $5y$ 3 $7p$ 4 q^3 5 $7g$ 6 $3g^2$

C   In the problems that follow, a choice of answers is given. Choose the correct one. Show how you make your choice.

Example:

Problem: I start with a number, add 5.4, the result is 15. What number did I start with?

Choose from 4, 6, 9.6, 11

Working: If I choose 4, then $4 + 5.4$ would give 9.4, not 15. So 4 cannot be the number I started with.

---

* Another way of saying that the value makes the equation true.

If I choose 6, then 6 + 5·4 would give 11·4, not 15. So 6 cannot be the number I started with.

If I choose 9·6, then 9·6 + 5·4 gives 15 which is right, so I must have started with 9·6.

1 I start with a number, subtract 7, the result is 4·73. What was the number? Choose from 17, 12·73, 11·73, 4·73.

2 I start with a number, multiply by 0·8, the result is 6·4. What was the number? Choose from 64, 1·6, 5·6, 8, 80.

3 I start with a number, divide by 4·5, the result is 20. What was the number? Choose from 9, 45, 90, 20.

4 I start with a number, add 3·26 and divide by 0·67, the result is 11·134 328. What was the number? Choose from 75, 44·132, 4·2, 42.

5 A bus had x passengers on board. At the next bus stop x new passengers got on and 3 got off. There were now 27 passengers on board. Find x. Choose from 40, 10, 15, 25.

6 A boy was given a bag of toffees by his uncle. His mother gave him another bag with the same number of toffees and his aunt gave him seven more. He had 35 toffees altogether, how many were in each bag? Choose from 10, 12, 14, 15.

Unit P26

Exercise P58

Work out the values of these expressions. Then check on the calculator. Where you get a different result make sure that you have used a correct sequence on the machine. Always work out the numbers in the brackets before anything else.

A
  1 $(4 + 5) \times 7$ 2 $(6 + 3) \times 5$ 3 $(10 + 5) \times 6$
  4 $(10 + 4) \times 5$ 5 $(6 - 3) \times 7$ 6 $(9 - 4) \times 2$
  7 $(8 - 3) \times 6$ 8 $(12 - 5) \times 4$ 9 $4 \times (6 + 4)$
  10 $9 \times (10 + 3)$ 11 $10 \times (5 + 2)$ 12 $8 \times (6 + 5)$
  13 $7 \times (3 - 3)$ 14 $9 \times (6 - 6)$ 15 $6 \times (5 - 4)$
  16 $10 \times (8 - 3)$

B
  1 $4 + (5 \times 7)$ 2 $6 + (3 \times 5)$ 3 $10 + (5 \times 6)$
  4 $10 + (4 \times 5)$ 5 $6 - (3 \times 7)$ 6 $9 - (4 \times 2)$
  7 $8 - (3 \times 6)$ 8 $12 - (5 \times 4)$ 9 $(4 \times 6) + 4$
  10 $(9 \times 10) + 3$ 11 $(10 \times 5) + 2$ 12 $(8 \times 6) + 5$
  13 $(7 \times 3) - 3$ 14 $(9 \times 6) - 6$ 15 $(6 \times 5) - 4$
  16 $(10 \times 8) - 3$

C
  1 $8 + (4 - 3)$ 2 $10 + (6 - 4)$ 3 $15 + (4 - 9)$
  4 $20 + (12 - 5)$ 5 $(8 + 6) - 5$ 6 $(10 + 3) - 8$
  7 $(12 + 8) - 4$ 8 $(20 + 10) - 5$ 9 $12 - (5 + 3)$
  10 $20 - (10 + 5)$ 11 $20 - (8 + 7)$ 12 $15 - (10 + 5)$
  13 $(14 - 7) + 5$ 14 $(18 - 9) + 3$ 15 $(20 - 7) + 7$
  16 $(19 - 8) + 9$

D
  1 $5 + (8 \div 4)$ 2 $7 - (6 \div 3)$ 3 $10 + (10 \div 2)$
  4 $12 - (9 \div 3)$ 5 $(6 + 8) \div 2$ 6 $(9 - 3) \div 3$
  7 $(14 - 9) \div 5$ 8 $(12 + 18) \div 10$ 9 $(10 \times 6) \div 2$
  10 $(8 \times 5) \div 4$ 11 $(7 \times 4) \div 2$ 12 $(10 \times 4) \div 5$
  13 $(12 \div 3) \times 4$ 14 $(15 \div 3) \times 2$ 15 $(20 \div 4) \times 3$
  16 $(24 \div 3) \times 5$

Exercise P59

A   Find the values of each of the following expressions given that $a = 1, b = 2, c = 3$.

1 $2a$	**2** $3a$	**3** $a + 2$
4 $2a + 1$	**5** $a + b$	**6** $3b + 1$
7 $a + 2b$	**8** $2a + b$	**9** $2a + 2b$
10 $3a + 2b$	**11** $a + 3b$	**12** $a + b + 3$
13 $a + b + c$	**14** $b + c$	**15** $b + c + a$
16 $2b + 3c$	**17** $2a + 2b + 2c$	**18** $3a + 3c$
19 $(a + b) + 3$	**20** $a + (b + 3)$	**21** $(a + b) \times 2$
22 $2(a + b)$	**23** $3(b + c)$	**24** $5(a + c)$
25 $3(a + b) + c$	**26** $2a + 3(b + c)$	**27** $a(b + c)$
28 $b(a + c)$		

B   Using the values $a = 2.3, b = 0.45$ and $c = 1.08$, and your calculator, find the values of these expressions.

1 $3a$	**2** $a + b$	**3** $a(b + 2)$
4 $b(a + 2)$	**5** $(a + b) + c$	**6** $a + (b + c)$
7 $3(a + b)$	**8** $2(a + b + c)$	**9** $(a + 4)(a + 5)$
10 $(a + 2)(b + 3)$	**11** $ab + ac$	**12** $a(b + c)$

C   Using the values $a = 270, b = 645$ and $c = 22$, and your calculator, show that:

1 $(a + b) - c$ is not equal to $a + (b - c)$

2 $2a$ is not equal to $2 + a$

3 $(a + b) \times c$ is not equal to $a + (b \times c)$

4 $ab + 4$ is not equal to $a(b + 4)$

5 $ab + bc$ is not equal to $a(b + c)$

6 $(a + b)(a + b)$ is not equal to $a^2 + b^2$

7 $(b + c) \times a$ is not equal to $b + (c \times a)$

8 $c(b + a)$ is not equal to $a(b + c)$

Exercise P60

A   Use brackets to describe what has happened to the number n.

1 n is multiplied by 5, and 6 is added to the result.

2   8 is subtracted from n and the result is multiplied by 4.

3   10 is added to n and the result is multiplied by 3.

4 n is doubled and 5 is then added.

5 n is divided by 6 and then 7 is subtracted.

6   5 is subtracted from n and the result is divided by 2.

7 Twice *n* has 6 added and the result is divided by 3.

8 4 is added to three times *n* and the result is divided by 3.

B What number is produced in the different parts of question **A** if:

   1 $n = 12$ **2** $n = 15$ **3** $n = 24$?

C Use brackets to make equations from this information and answer the question.

   1 A boy buying a bicycle pays £10 each month and then a further £17. Altogether he pays £97. How many months does he pay the £10? (Start with *n* months.)

   2 A girl working on a farm gets double wages per hour on Saturdays and Sundays. She works 7 hours during the week and 12 hours at the weekend. She earns £12·40. What is her rate per hour on weekdays? (Start with *n* pence per hour.)

   3 Two children found a purse of money in the park and gave it to the police. After three months, as no one had claimed the purse, they were allowed to keep the money. They gave £4 to charity and shared the rest. If they each had £5·50, how much was in the purse? (Start with £*n* in the purse.)

   4 A rectangle has one side 5 cm longer than the other. The perimeter (all the way round) is 28 cm. What are the lengths of the sides of the rectangle? (Start with the shorter side being *n* cm long.)

Unit P27

Exercise P61

A In the diagrams below each of the smaller triangles has been enlarged into the bigger one. Find the scale factor and use it to find the length of the side marked ?. Check by measurement.

1

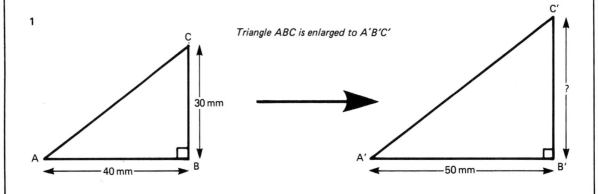

Triangle ABC is enlarged to A'B'C'

2

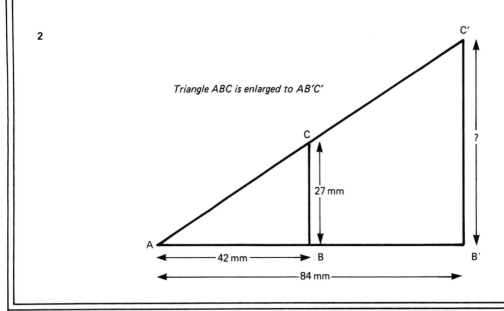

Triangle ABC is enlarged to AB'C'

3

Triangle ABC is enlarged to AB'C'

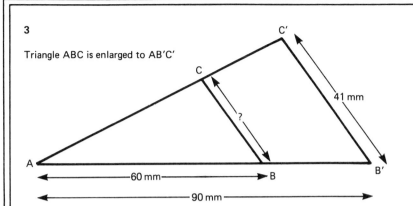

B **1** Draw a set of six different triangles whose angles are 72°, 72° and 36°. Draw the base first and then use your protractor to draw the sides at 72° to the base.

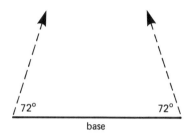

Measure the triangles and complete this table.

△	Length of base	Length of long side	Height	Long side ÷ base	Height ÷ base
1					
2					
3					
4					
5					
6					

What do you notice?

2 Use your protractor to draw five different triangles with angles 25°, 65° and 90°.

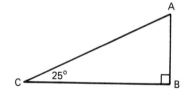

Complete this table for the five triangles.

△	Length AB	Length BC	Length CA	$\dfrac{AC}{AB}$	$\dfrac{AC}{BC}$	$\dfrac{BC}{AC}$
1						
2						
3						
4						
5						

3 Repeat question **2** but this time choose your own angles for the triangles. Draw and measure carefully.

Exercise P62

Some measurements of the animals in the pictures are given below. Work out the scale of each picture and use it to find another measurement for each animal.

Elephant   4·0 m (high)
Flea   2·5 mm (long)
Whale   20·0 m (long)
Amoeba   0·3 mm (left to right)
Cyclops   1·5 mm (body length)
Squid   60·0 cm (long)

elephant

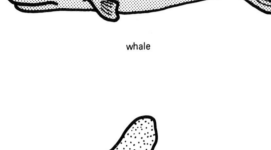

whale

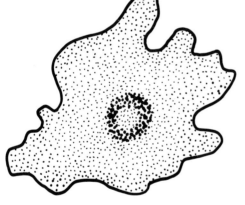

amoeba

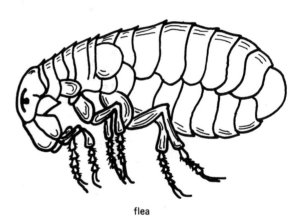

flea

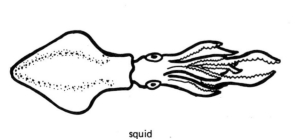

squid

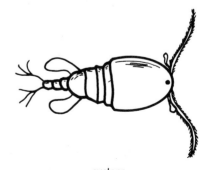

cyclops